BAR INTERNATIONAL SERIES 3101 | 2022

Late Antiquity and Early Christianity in the Roman Provinces of Moesia Prima and Dacia Ripensis

OLIVERA ILIĆ

Published in 2022 by
BAR Publishing, Oxford, UK

BAR International Series 3101

Late Antiquity and Early Christianity in the Roman Provinces of Moesia Prima and Dacia Ripensis

ISBN 978 1 4073 6033 1   paperback
ISBN 978 1 4073 6034 8   e-format

DOI https://doi.org/10.30861/9781407360331

A catalogue record for this book is available from the British Library

© Olivera Ilić 2022

COVER IMAGE *Panjevac near Ćuprija. A bronze lamp with the handle in the shape of the head of a griffin. (National Museum of Serbia)*

The Author's moral rights under the 1988 UK Copyright, Designs and Patents Act are hereby expressly asserted.

All rights reserved. No part of this work may be copied, reproduced, stored, sold, distributed, scanned, saved in any form of digital format or transmitted in any form digitally, without the written permission of the Publisher.

Links to third party websites are provided by BAR Publishing in good faith and for information only. BAR Publishing disclaims any responsibility for the materials contained in any third-party website referenced in this work.

BAR titles are available from:

BAR Publishing
122 Banbury Rd, Oxford, OX2 7BP, UK
info@barpublishing.com
www.barpublishing.com

Of Related Interest

Le c.d. gammadiae nelle catacombe cristiane di Roma
Censimento, confronti ed ipotesi interpretative
Cristina Cumbo
BAR International Series **2947** | 2019

Patrimonio Culturale, Paesaggi e Personaggi dell'altopiano ibleo
Scritti di archeologia e museologia della Sicilia sud-orientale
Santino Alessandro Cugno con il contributo di Ray Bondin, Franco Dell'Aquila, Iorga Ivano Prato, Paolo Daniele Scirpo e la prefazione di Lorenzo Guzzardi
BAR International Series **2874** | 2017

Mosaici tardoantichi dell'isola di Cos
Scavi italiani 1912–1945
Lorella Maria De Matteis
BAR International Series **2515** | 2013

Conimbriga tardo-antigua y medieval
Excavaciones arqueológicas en la domus tancinus (2004–2008) (Condeixa-a-Velha, Portugal)
Jorge López Quiroga
BAR International Series **2466** | 2013

Las necrópolis urbanas
Las necrópolis urbanas
Isabel Sánchez Ramos
BAR International Series **2126** | 2010

Late Roman African Urbanism
Continuity and Transformation in the City
Gareth Sears
BAR International Series **1693** | 2007

The Christianisation of Malta
Catacombs, cult centres and churches in Malta to 1530
Mario Buhagiar
BAR International Series **1674** | 2007

Pagans and Christians - from Antiquity to the Middle Ages
Papers in honour of Martin Henig, presented on the occasion of his 65th birthday
Edited by Lauren Gilmour
BAR International Series **1610** | 2007

Provincial Cilicia and the Archaeology of Temple Conversion
Richard Bayliss
BAR International Series **1281** | 2004

Christianity in Roman Pannonia
An evaluation of Early Christian finds and sites from Hungary
Dorottya Gáspár
BAR International Series **1010** | 2002

For more information, or to purchase these titles, please visit **www.barpublishing.com**

Acknowledgements

On this occasion I would like to express my very grateful thanks to:

Miomir Korać, director of the Institute of Archaeology in Belgrade and the director of the antique project *Viminacium, Roman City and Military Camp*, for his cooperation and encouragement, and for giving me the financial and personal support that made this work possible and without which I could not have completed my research.

I would also like to thank my colleagues: Miroslav Vujović, Professor of the Department of Archaeology, Faculy of Philosophy in Belgrade, Bojana Borić-Bresković, director of the National Museum of Serbia, Maja Živić, curator of the Museum in Zaječar who presented me with archaeological material from their museum collections and for their generous help.

My thanks also go to the following colleagues: Gordana Jeremić (Institute of Archaeology in Belgrade), Nika Strugar (Belgrade City Museum), Dragana Spasić-Djurić (National Museum in Požarevac), Tatjana Gačpar (Museum in Smederevo), Gordan Janjić (Krajina Museum in Negotin). Special thanks go to Aleksandra Subotić for her help with the arrangement of illustrative material in the book.

My grateful thanks go to the editor, Jacqueline Senior, for encouraging and supporting me in publishing this book.

Contents

List of Figures ix
Abbreviations xi
Abstract xiii

1. Introduction 1
    1.1. Research of early Christianity in the area of the central Balkans 1
    1.2. The beginning of Christianisation 2

2. Sacral Architecture 7
    2.1. Churches 7
    2.2. Chapels 17
    2.3. Baptisteries 19

3. Objects Used in Early Christian Liturgical Rites 23
    3.1. Liturgical vessels 24
    3.2. Censers 26
    3.3. Spoons 31
    3.4. Processional crosses 33

4. Objects Related to Christian Cult 35
    4.1. Reliquaries 35
    4.2. Gilded glass base 36

5. Church Inventory 39
    5.1. Polycandela 39
    5.2. Candelabra 41
    5.3. Lamps 42

6. Objects of Profane Character with Christian Symbols 51
    6.1. Artistic objects 51
    6.2. Jewellery 51
    6.3. Decorative objects of clothing and military equipment 54
    6.4. Utilitarian objects 55

7. Funeral Rites 59

8. Conclusion 65

Catalogue 67
Ancient Sources 77
Bibliography 79

List of Figures

Figure 1.1. Gamzigrad–*Romuliana*. General view of the palace 6

Map 2.1. The Early Christian sites with sacral architecture in the provinces of *Moesia Prima* and *Dacia Ripensis* 7

Figure 2.1. Kostolac–*Viminacium*. Plan of the city and legionary camp 9

Figure 2.2. Gamzigrad–*Romuliana*. Basilica I and basilica II in the southern part of the Late Antique palace 10

Figure 2.3. Gamzigrad–*Romuliana*. Plan of the three-nave basilica II 10

Figure 2.4. Gamzigrad–*Romuliana*. Plan of the church and baptistery in the eastern part of the Late Antique palace 11

Figure 2.5. Čezava–*Novae*. Plan of the fortification and the church 12

Figure 2.6. Čezava–*Novae*. The church from the 6th century, detail 13

Figure 2.7. Boljetin–*Smorna*. General view of the fortification and the church 13

Figure 2.8. Boljetin–*Smorna*. Plan of the fortification and the church 14

Figure 2.9. Boljetin–*Smorna*. Early Christian church, ground plan 14

Figure 2.10. a-b. Boljetin–*Smorna*. a) apse with the baptistery; b) detail of the baptistery 15

Figure 2.11. Donji Milanovac–*Taliata*. Plan of the fortification and the church 16

Figure 2.12. Donji Milanovac–*Taliata*. Early Christian church, ground plan 16

Figure 2.13. Donji Milanovac–*Taliata*. A baptistery erected inside the previous tower, detail 17

Figure 2.14. Saldum. Plan of the fortification with a tower used as a chapel 18

Figure 2.15. Saldum. NE tower – chapel, ground plan 18

Figure 2.16. Donje Butorke. Plan of the fortification with a tower used as a chapel 19

Map 3.1. The sites with Early Christian findings in the provinces of *Moesia Prima* and *Dacia Ripensis* 23

Figure 3.1. Kostolac–*Viminacium*. Collection of silver chalices (5) 24

Figure 3.2. Kostolac–*Viminacium*. Silver bowl with Christ monogram 25

Figure 3.3. a-b Kostolac–*Viminacium*. Silver bowls with two stamps in the form of Latin cross (2) 26

Figure 3.4. Unknown site. Silver bowl with monogram 26

Figure 3.5. a-c Kostol–*Pontes*. Bronze pitcher, view and details 27

Figure 3.6. a-d Gamzigrad–*Romuliana*. A hoard of church items: a – polycandelon; b – candelabrum; c – censer; d – mushroom-shaped fittings 28

Figure 3.7. a-b Kuršumlija, Pepeljevac. Bronze censer with relief depictions from the life of Christ 30

Figure 3.8. Kostolac–*Viminacium*. Silver spoons 32

Figure 3.9. Gamzigrad–*Romuliana*. Processional cross 34

Figure 4.1. Gamzigrad–*Romuliana*. Silver reliquary 36

Figure 4.2. Prahovo–*Aquae*. Gilded glass base.. 36

Figure 5.1. Gamzigrad–*Romuliana*. Glass lamps – parts of polycandela 41

Figure 5.2. Panjevac near Ćuprija. A bronze lamp with the handle in the shape of the head of a griffin 43

Figure 5.3. Belgrade–*Singidunum*. Bronze lamp with a cross-like handle 45

Figure 5.4. Smederevo (Mezul)–*Vinceia*. Bronze lamp in the form of a ship 45

Figure 5.5. Smederevo, Mezul site–*Vinceia*. Bronze lamp in the form of ship 46

Figure 5.6. Belgrade–*Singidunum*. Pottery lamp with two figures and crosses 48

Figure 5.7. Saldum fort. Pottery lamp with a cross and a handle in the form of a palmette 48

Figure 5.8. Prahovo–*Aquae*. Pottery lamp with a cross–shaped handle 49

Figure 6.1. Smederevo–*Vinceia*. A statuette of the Good Shepherd 51

Figure 6.2. Višnjica–*Ad Octavum*. Gold necklace with two medallions and a cross 52

Figure 6.3. Kostolac–*Viminacium*, Više Grobalja site. Pendant in the shape of a cross 53

Figure 6.4. a-c Gamzigrad–*Romuliana*. Three cross-shaped pendants 53

Figure 6.5. Unknown site. Gold finger ring with Christian symbols 54

Figure 6.6. Kostolac–*Viminacium*, Pećine site. Silver ring with Christogram 54

Figure 6.7. Prahovo–*Aquae*. Bronze cross–shaped fibula with Christogram 55

Figure 6.8. Kostolac–*Viminacium*, Čair site. Application of helmet with *Chi-Ro* motif 56

Figure 6.9. Manastir site, Danube limes. Application of helmet with *Chi-Ro* motif 56

Figure 6.10. Belgrade–*Singidunum*. Bronze stamp in the form of a cross 56

Figure 6.11. a) Belgrade–*Singidunum*. Bronze steelyard and counterweight. (Documentation of the Belgrade City Museum). b) Belgrade–*Singidunum*. Counterweight shaped like the bust of a Byzantine Empress 57

Figure 6.12/1. Saldum fort. Amphora with a cross painted in red. 2, 3. Boljetin–*Smorna*. Amphorae with crosses painted in red. 4. Donji Milanovac–*Taliata*. Amphora with cross painted in red 57

Figure 7.1. Belgrade–*Singidunum*. The so-called Jonah sarcophagus 60

Figure 7.2. a-c Kostolac–*Viminacium*, the site of Pećine (G/5517). Christogram with the apocalyptical letters α and ω in the painted Christian tomb 61

Figure 7.3. Kostolac–*Viminacium*, the site of Pećine (G/5517). Representation of the Garden of Eden in the painted Christian tomb 61

Figure 7.4. Kostolac–*Viminacium*, the site of Pećine. Brick with the engraved Christogram 61

Figure 7.5. a-d Kostolac–*Viminacium*. Early Christian inscriptions 62

Abbreviations

AV	Arheološki vestnik, Ljubljana
Glasnik SAD	Glasnik Srpskog arheološkog društva, Beograd
Glas SANU	Glas Srpske akademije nauka i umetnosti, Beograd
Glas SKA	Glas Srpske Kraljevske Akademije, Beograd
Glasnik ZMS	Glasnik Zemaljskog muzeja, Sarajevo
Godišnjak GB	Godišnjak grada Beograda, Beograd
Spomenik SAN	Spomenik Srpske Akademije nauka, Beograd
Spomenik SKA	Spomenik Srpske Kraljevske Akademije, Beograd
VAMZ	Vjesnik Arheološkog muzeja u Zagrebu, Zagreb
Vesnik VM	Vesnik Vojnog muzeja, Beograd
Zbornik FF	Zbornik Filozofskog fakulteta u Beogradu, Beograd
Zbornik NM	Zbornik Narodnog muzeja, Beograd
Zbornik radova NM	Zbornik radova Narodnog muzeja, Beograd
ZRVI	Zbornik radova Vizantološkog instituta, Beograd
ŽA	Živa antika, Skoplje

Abstract

The beginning and development of early Christianity along the Middle Danube Limes, in the Roman provinces of *Moesia Prima* and *Dacia Ripensis*, as well as cities and fortifications in the hinterland of the Limes during the two main stages of Late Antiquity and early Byzantine period are documented in literary sources and archaeological data. Our present knowledge of the spiritual life of the inhabitants of cities and fortifications in the Middle Danube Limes in Late Antiquity shows that, besides the dominance of the official religion of Rome, the importance of Christianity was increasing, as evidenced by the preserved material remains. The new religion and changes that occurred in the cultural life of the autochthonous Romanised population can best be seen in the architecture and its most common forms. By the fourth century, Christianity had become an official Roman religion, and a new architectural form, the basilica, would soon become the standard throughout the Roman world. Aside from monumental basilicas, which dominated in every more or less urbanised centre, smaller church edifices were also erected in areas that were more isolated, geographically, from their political and religious centres. The number and variety of sacral architecture and objects of a religious character devoted to liturgical practice, as well as objects of a profane nature with clear Christian features that are represented both in larger urban structures and in fortifications on the Middle Danube Limes, indicate the existence of a well organised Christian church and an already developed form of Christian life in these areas in the period from the 4th to the beginning of the 7th century.

Keywords: Late Antiquity, early Byzantine period, Christianisation, sacral architecture, religious artefacts, *Moesia Prima*, *Dacia Ripensis*, Middle Danube Limes.

Introduction

The Late Antiquity period, which continues chronologically into the period of the Early Empire, was filled with tumultuous events and turmoils that brought deep political, economic and social changes in the Roman Empire, leading to a gradual feudalisation of society. This period has long been recognised among scholars as a period of large political, religious and cultural changes, which determined the later history of the Mediterranean region and Europe. The Christian religion, which appeared as a bearer of new ideas and a new philosophy, transformed into the bearer of dominant social and cultural life and became a political factor that caused a radical change in the foundations of the social system. By widening and fortifying its political power in the area of the Balkan Peninsula, the Roman Empire created conditions that would allow, somewhat later, the spread of Christianity. The new church adjusted its organisation to the administrative organisation of the state, thus, the main cities of the Roman provinces would become, at the same time, new ecclesiastic seats as well.

At the first half of the 4th century the possibility of free confession of faith, brought prosperity and progress to Christianity, both in terms of the organisation of the Church itself, but also in terms of architectonic and artistic development as well. At that time, larger urban centres got their first basilicas, along with minor cities and fortifications as well. Outside of the city walls (*extra muros*), necropolises were being formed, which churches dedicated to the cult of the dead.

Monuments from the Late Antique period that are determined into the early Christian period indicate its creative force and importance in the religious, social and economic life of that time. In order to create a clearer image of the real importance of Christianity and the role it played in the area of the Danube provinces of *Moesia Prima* and *Dacia Ripensis*, i.e. the north-eastern part of the prefecture of Illyricum (*Praefectura praetorio per Illyricum*), we will provide an overview of archaeological monuments and items known so far that have distinctly Christian attributes. Aside from archaeological findings, historical sources have also contributed to a fuller overview of the Early Christian period, its prevalence and spread, as well as to the attempt to provide an answer to the question as to who its representatives were. The chronological timeframe that encompasses Late Antiquity has not been strictly defined, although the time from the beginning of the 4th century up until the middle of the 7th century is recognised by most scholars as the period in which Late Antiquity traits were most conspicuous and in which the Christian religion acquired its final form, and grew into a strong religious system that began to increasingly influence the change of the system of the state and the society.

1.1. Research of early Christianity in the area of the central Balkans

Systematic research of the sites in the provinces of *Moesia Prima* and *Dacia Ripensis*, particulary along the Middle Danube Limes, represented by important urban and military centres, enables an insight into the processes of Christianisation through the remains of church architecture, sepulchral monuments, as well as the different objects used in the Christian cult or personal piety. Among the first writers and researchers of Early Christian monuments in the territory of central Balkans (today's Serbia), a special place is held by Arthur Evans, who amassed a vast amount of data on his travels through Serbia at the end of the 19th century.[1] Felix Kanitz focused his interests in the field of archaeology on the Danube Limes and, therefore, he remains, even today, after more than one century and numerous destructions, both natural ones and those caused by human factors, one of the most important sources for studying the cultural heritage of this part of the Balkans.[2] His extensive research and observations provided a foundation for many later archaeological research activities, especially for the large-scale archaeological excavations within the projects Iron Gates I and Iron Gates II, which lasted from the 1960s up to the beginning of the 1980s. Having examined all the material he left us in this field, we may freely place him among the most important researchers of the cultural heritage of Antiquity in the territory of Serbia.

A figure that also stands out among the prominent researchers in Serbia is Mihailo Valtrović, the founder of Serbian archaeology and the first professor at the then newly founded Department of Archaeology at the Great School in Belgrade, who was also the director of the National Museum in Belgrade (1881). From the 1880s, Mihailo Valtrović started publishing studies about Early Christian churches, tombs, sarcophagi and different early Christian artefacts.[3] Further investigations in *Viminacium* were continued by Miloje Vasić, at the beginning of the

---

[1] A. Evans was one of the first researchers of antiquities in the territory of central Balkans: Evans, A. *Antiquariens Researches in Illyricum* IV. Westminster 1883.
[2] The book is an important source of data for later researchers: Kanitz, F. *Römische Studien in Serbien. Der Donau-Grenzwall, das Strassennetz, die Städte, Castelle, Denkmale, Thermen und Bergwerke zur Römerzeit im Königreiche Serbien*. Wien 1892.
[3] Valtrović Mihailo recorded the existence of a rich fresco-painted tomb in *Viminacium*, which was destroyed by the locals, see: Valtrović, M.

20th century, who developed the first known typology of burial forms in *Viminacium*.[4] Vladimir Petković, who continued Vasić's work, even though he was an art historian, had great success in his work dealing with Late Antique and Early Christian archaeology as well. From the very beginning of his work, he displayed an interest in Early Christian archaeology, starting from his PhD thesis, entitled *Ein frühchristliches Elfenbeinrelief im Nationalmuseum zu München* (1905), and also somewhat later, on his return from Munich, when he wrote the article about Early Christian sarcophagus from Belgrade.[5] Thanks to him, the research of Caričin Grad (*Iustiniana Prima*) began, not long before the Balkan Wars (1912).[6] Later, in the period between the two World Wars, he was the head of excavations on this site (1937–1939).

The greatest stimulus in discovering the monuments from the early Christian epoch was at the time of extensive archaeological works in the course of the construction of the Djerdap I hydroelectric power plant during the 1960s and 1970s. As part of the research of the forts' interiors and their immediate surroundings, the remains of foundations of several churches, chapels and tombs were also examined. Archaeological material from the Early Christian period was also found, though it was somewhat scarce.[7]

A considerable contribution to the research of Early Christian archaeology and history was also provided by Vladislav Popović, in his numerous articles published in local and foreign journals.[8] Ivanka Nikolajević showed a special interest in her papers for the topic of Late Antique and Early Christian art, especially relief and decorations,[9] as well as the issue of burials in this period.[10]

Gordana Marjanović-Vujović dedicated several of her papers to the Early Christian period, to crucifixes[11] and polycandela[12] from the Collection of the National Museum in Belgrade. Branka Jeličić also published papers of Early Christian items from the Collection of the National Museum in Belgrade.[13] Mirjana Tatić-Djurić provided a significant contribution to the research of the Early Christian period in the area of the province of *Moesia Prima*, from which a paper on silver vessels from *Viminacium* particularly stands out.[14] In recent years, a series of individual papers, studies, and catalogues of findings were published that complete our knowledge of religious life in the period of Late Antiquity.[15]

1.2. The beginning of Christianisation

In the Roman Empire, religion was intricately linked to the state, i.e. the supreme governing power, due to the fact that the emperor, as the highest priest (*pontifex maximus*), was required to take care of the religion of the state. The religious concept of Rome was imposed on conquered peoples as well, who accepted it, along with other forms of Romanisation, adapting local beliefs to the official religion. The cult of Roman gods would soon gain supporters among the urban population, while the local population in the rural and mountainous regions would attribute the functions of their old gods to the Roman deities, through the process of *interpretatio Romana*.

With the ascension of Diocletian to the throne, and the establishment of the Tetrarchy, significant religious and ideological changes occurred in Roman society. Rulers such as Diocletian, Maximian Herculius, Galerius and Constantius Chlorus, became members of the family of Jupiter and Hercules (*Iovii et Herculii*), believing themselves to be the emissaries of gods, being bearers of their name and nature. The period of the First Tetrarchy, most prominently the reign of Diocletian and Galerius, was marked by vicious persecutions of the Christians. The persecutions reached their culmination after the fourth edict against the Christians, issued by Diocletian in 304 AD (Bratož 2003, 42–43, 71–85). Galerius, who became the Augustus after the meeting in *Carnuntum* (308 AD), was in *Serdica*, together with Maxentius, in the spring of 311 AD, and was severely ill (Lact., *Mort. Persc.* XXXIII, 7). Several days before his death, Galerius issued an edict which guaranteed Christians from all over the Empire the freedom to practice their religion. Even though this legal act, because of the death of Galerius and unstable situation in the Empire, had no important direct consequences, it certainly marked an important step towards the enabling

---

Starohrišćanski sarkofag nađen u Beogradu, *Starinar* III, Beograd 1886, 70–71. Valtrović, M. Dobri pastir, *Starinar* VIII, Beograd 1891, 109–130.

[4] The first archeological excavations at *Viminacium* was started by Miloje Vasić at the beginning of the 20th century, see: Vasić, M. Nekolike grobne konstrukcije iz Viminacijuma, *Starinar* n.r. II, Beograd 1907, 66–98.

[5] Petković, V. Jedan rani hrišćanski sarkofag iz Beograda, *Glas SKA* LXXII, 1907, 186–219.

[6] Excavations at Caričin Grad, begun by Vladislav Petković, meant, at the same time, the beginning of the expansion of archaeology of the paleo-Byzantine period. Numerous architectonic monuments dedicated to the cult, and also the accompanying church inventory, represent, at the same time, important findings of Early Christian archaeology as well.

[7] The papers were published in the journals *Arheološki pregled* 1964–1970, and *Starinar* 33–34 (1982–1983), 1984.

[8] Popović, V. Ranohrišćanska bronzana lampa iz okoline Smedereva, *Starinar* XX, 1970, 323–330; V. Popović, Grčki natpis iz Caričinog Grada i pitanje ubikacije Prve Justinijane, *Glas SANU* CCCLX, knj. 7, 1990, 53–108.

[9] Nikolajević, I. Ranovizantijska arhitektonska dekorativna plastika u Makedoniji, Srbiji i Crnoj Gori, Beograd 1957; *Eadem.*, Les monuments de la décoration architecturale en Serbie d'un atelier local du VIe siècle, *Actes du Ve Congrès International d'archéologie chrétienne*, Roma–Paris 1957, 567–571. *Eadem.*, Nekoliko ranohrišćanskih reljefa geometrijskog stila iz Dalmacije, *ZRVI* XI, Beograd 1968, 15–27; *Eadem.*, Ranohrišćanske krstionice u Jugoslaviji, *ZRVI* IX, 1966, 223–255.

[10] Nikolajević, I. Sahranjivanje u ranohrišćanskim crkvama na području Srbije, *AV* 29, Ljubljana 1978, 678–693.

[11] Marjanović-Vujović, G. *Krstovi od VI do XII veka iz zbirke Narodnog muzeja*, Beograd, 1977.

[12] Marjanović-Vujović, G. Dva rana hrišćanska polijeleja iz Narodnog muzeja, *Zbornik NM* VII, 1973, 13–23.

[13] Jeličić, B. Bronzani žišci u Narodnom muzeju, *Zbornik radova NM* II, 1959, 73–82; Jeličić, B. Bronzani kandelabr u Narodnom muzeju u Beogradu, *Zbornik NM* IV, 1964, 151–155.

[14] Tatić-Đurić, M. Srebrno posuđe iz Kostolca, *Zbornik NM* V, 1967, 237–246.

[15] Kondić, J. Ranovizantijsko srebro, u: *Antičko srebro u Srbiji*, I. Popović (ur.), Beograd 1994, 65–67; Ilić, O. Early Christian Baptistries in Northern Illyricum, *Starinar* LVI, 2008, 223–244; *Konstantin Veliki i Milanski edikt 313*, katalog izložbe povodom 1700 godina Milanskog edikta, Beograd: Narodni muzej 2013.

Christians to realise the right to their faith, representing a new step in a series of pieces of legislation.

Christianity was not merely a new religious system or a powerful religious passion in a time of crisis, instead, it also appeared as a bearer of new ideas, a new philosophy, and it became a political factor that conditioned a radical change of the system of both the state and society. Having appeared in times of difficult political and economic crises, when old religious and moral principles were in decay and abandoned, Christianity acquired a large number of supporters in the masses, gaining a messianic importance. As a new universal religion, it was proclaimed a *religio illicita* by the Empire and such a position caused a period of persecutions of the Christians, which lasted all the way until Constantine the Great.

The Christian church adjusted its organisation to the administrative organisation of the state and, hence, the capitals of the Roman provinces also became episcopal seats at the same time, and the actual organisation of the church was subordinated to the political division of the provinces. The rise and the fall of church life in the territory of the Balkans was directly linked to the changeable political circumstances that the provinces of this area were exposed to. The area of the Diocese of Dacia, i.e. Northern Illyricum, came into contact with the new religion at a later point than the southern part of the Balkans, where Christianity had been present ever since the times of the apostles. According to the scriptures of the New Testament, it was Paul the Apostle and his followers that preached Christianity in these areas, while founding the first church communities.[16] In one of his Epistles to the Romans, Paul the Apostle says that he came as far as the Illyrian lands while preaching; it is assumed that this did not refer to the lands around the Danube, but the Mediterranean lands instead, where communities already existed to which he could preach (Zeiller 1918 (rp. 1967), 27–28). The coasts of the Aegean, Ionian and Adriatic Sea, with their cities, became centres from which Christianity spread further on towards the inner regions of the Balkans. Paul the Apostle, in his Epistles, and Luke the Apostle and Evangelist, in the Acts of the Apostles, speak of the first Christian communities in larger urban settlements, from which we can conclude that the beginnings of Christianity should be sought in urban agglomerations of the Balkan Peninsula first. This is the reason why certain scholars call Christianity the "religion of the cities" (Lebreton et Zeiller 1946, 16–17). The Christianisation process was considerably slower in the mountainous hinterland and deeper in the inner parts of the Balkan peninsula, due to the greater isolation of the population from the main communication routes.

In the first centuries of the new era, Roman historians rarely mention Christianity in the northern part of the prefecture of Illyricum. The first reports on the presence of Christians in the Danube Valley come from the times of Marcus Aurelius (161–180) and his war against the Quadi. The war was fought by a legion that was brought in from the East (*Legio XII Fulminata*), in which there was a considerable number of Christians, as noted by Tertullian (Migne, *PL* I, 450) and Eusebius of Caesarea (Migne, *PL* XX, 442). Reliable reports on the first persecutions of Christians in the area of Northern Illyricum come only from the times of Diocletian. Four edicts issued on the topic (303–304 AD) claimed numerous victims from the territory comprehended by the provinces of *Moesia Prima* and, further down the Danube, *Dacia Ripensis*, and *Dacia Mediterranea* in the south-east. Among the persecuted individuals, there were members of the Roman army stationed along the Danube (Zeiller 1918 (rp. 1967), 59). These persecutions bear witness on the presence of Christians in the area of the Diocese of Dacia at the beginning of the 4th century. Most Christian martyrs noted by sources or tradition were linked to larger urban centres in these provinces.

Some of the important cities in the provinces of *Moesia Prima* and *Dacia Ripensis* were *Viminacium*, the capital of the province of *Moesia Prima*, *Singidunum* and *Margum*. In the province of *Dacia Ripensis*, *Aquae* and *Romuliana* represented important ecclesiastic seats. Aside from those, traces of the Early Christian period are also present in Roman fortifications along the Danube Limes: church buildings, baptisteries, chapels, and other archaeological finds.[17]

Singidunum

One of the important cities in the province of *Moesia Prima* was *Singidunum* (today Belgrade). As a fortification in the border area, it was the seat of the *Legio IV Flavia*, which was stationed in the Danube Valley during the times of Domitian, in 86 AD, but it was moved to *Singidunum* during the reign of Trajan (Mirković 1968, 37–49). Because of its exceptional strategic importance, being located at the confluence of the river Sava and the Danube, the city came into the possession of various tribes and tribal alliances that inhabited these areas, especially during the 5th century. According to sources from that time, we learn that the city was partially restored after the fall of the Hun state in 454 AD, only to be conquered by the Sarmatians later, who would lose it, in turn, to the Goths of Theodoric in 471 AD. The Goths would abandon the city in ca 488 AD, when they headed to the west, to Italy, hence, the city would come under the administrative government of Eastern Rome again (Barišić 1955b, 2–3). Even though Procopius says that *Singidunum* remained in

---

[16] The scriptures of the New Testament contain the Epistle of Paul the Apostle directed to Christian communities in cities in the south of the Balkan Peninsula: one to the Philippians, in Macedonia, two to the Christians in Thessaloniki, two to Corinth, in Achaia, and one to Titus the Apostle, on the island of Crete. *Cf.* Lebreton J. et Zeiller, J. *L'Eglise primitive* I, Paris 1946, 176–188. Acts of the Apostles, 16, 9–12; 17, 1–14; 19, 21–22; 20, 1–2.

[17] The focus of our research are cities and fortifications located in the territory of today's Serbia. The Early Christian period in the part of the province of *Dacia Ripensis* located in today's Bulgaria, among which is the capital of this province, *Ratiaria*, will not be taken into consideration.

ruins throughout the entire period from Attila to Justinian, events linked to Theodoric's invasion of Srem in 504 AD, and especially the Byzantine–Goth treaty from 510 AD, clearly indicate that the newly created political situation was unfavourable for Byzantium and, in this context, indicate the strategic importance of the city because of the newly created Goth province of *Pannonia Secunda*. Under such circumstances, the conclusion of certain historians that Emperor Anastasius (491–518) restored the fortress at the confluence of the Sava and the Danube just before the year of 510 AD, if not before, seems only logical (Barišić 1955a, 66–67). Justinian I had certainly already started, at the beginning of his reign, works on the restoration of *Singidunum*, as can be clearly seen from *Novella XI* from 535 AD, where *Moesia Prima* is treated as an already organised region. Procopius informs us of this, and continuing the already mentioned report on the devastation of the city by the Huns, says: "Emperor Justinian rebuilt it (*Singidunum*) entirely, surrounded it with a strong wall, and again made it a noble and admirable city" (Procop. *De Aedif.* IV 5, p. 269). The Avar–Slav attacks and the siege of the city, which lasted from 579 to 582 AD, historical sources mention a military commander named Sethos, who, along with the bishop of *Singidunum*, strived to defend not only *Singidunum*, but *Sirmium* as well (Barišić 1955a, 92–93). The city was still under Byzantine government in the time of Phocas (602–610), judging by the fact that there are no reports on Avar-Slav intrusions in this part of the Danube Valley from this period. The report by Porphyrogenitus regarding the time of the reign of Heraclius (610–641), from which it can be seen that the city was still under Byzantine government even in ca 630 AD, represents the final known piece of information on *Singidunum* (Barišić 1955b, 12, note 52).

The Christians of *Singidunum* are first mentioned during the persecutions of Emperor Diocletian.[18] Among the first Christian martyrs mentioned by sources is deacon Donatus, *diaconicus sanctae ecclesiae Singidoniensis*. The death of a group of Christians from *Singidunum* is also mentioned, including a priest Montanus and his wife Maxima (Zeiller 1918 (rp. 1967), 75–76, 78). Somewhat later, two more martyrs are mentioned, also from *Singidunum*. These were the martyrs Hermylus and Stratonicus, who were executed after the year 313 AD (Popović 1991, 73–80). Their bodies were thrown into the Danube and buried 18 miles downstream of *Singidunum*, as mentioned in the insufficiently reliable work of Monologium by Metaphrast, at the point where the fortification of *Aureus Mons* was located possibly in the area of today's village of Brestovik, (Mirković 1979, 21). One Roman tomb was discovered there, dated to the 3rd–4th century (Milošević 2017, 7–24), however, there was another, later phase, when an additional chamber with apses, a porch and an entry hall, was added to the original compartment (Mirković 1979, 23).

Ursacius was among the first bishops of *Singidunum*, who participated in the Council of Tyre in 335 AD, as an opponent of Bishop Athanasius of Alexandria, one of the leading exponents of the Nicene doctrine (Zeiller 1918 (rp. 1967), 149–150). In his time, the Episcopal see of *Singidunum* had an important role in church politics and the spread of Arianism, which was present in the territory of Northern Illyricum. Bishop Ursacius is also linked to the severe conflict with representatives of the Nicene doctrine, and after the first Ecumenical Council in *Nicaea* in 325 AD, along with Valens, the bishop of *Mursa*, he would be one of the most prominent exponents of Arianism. The Council of *Serdica,* in 343 AD, was supposed to make peace between these two opposing dogmatic views, however, the discord between their representatives only increased. The bishop of *Singidunum* remained a stern opponent of the Nicene dogma. The councils held in *Sirmium* in the period from 351 to 358 AD made Northern Illyricum the centre of religious conflicts in the middle of the 4th century. A local Synod of representatives of Arianism was held in *Singidunum*. A letter and a delegation were sent from the Council to the bishop of *Sirmium*, demanding that he remain faithful to the teachings of Arius (Zeiller 1918 (rp. 1967), 304–306). After Ursacius, Bishop Secundianus ascended to the Episcopal see of *Singidunum*, and he also continued the stern fight against the opponents of Arianism. He would be condemned at the Council in *Aquileia* in 381 AD, along with Bishop Paladius from *Ratiaria* (Popović 1995, 195). In conclusion, we can say that the history of Arianism is closely linked to the area of Illyricum and, therefore, *Singidunum* as well. There are no written testimonies on the later bishops of *Singidunum*. According to Justinian's Novella CXXXI, the episcopal see still existed in the 6th century. Here, the regions that were under the jurisdiction of the newly founded archbishopric also included the territory of *Moesia Prima*, leading us to assume that the episcopal sees of *Singidunum* and *Viminacium* had already been restored in this period (Zeiller 1918 (rp. 1967), 151).

Margum

The Roman fortified city of *Margum* lies on the right bank of the river Morava, near its confluence with the Danube. It is mentioned by the historian Priscus while talking about the Byzantine-Hun negotiations during the reign of Theodosius II (Barišić 1955b, 9). According to his testimony, the Huns attacked the fortifications along the Danube Limes in 434 because the bishop of the city of *Margum*, whose name remains unknown, came into their territory and stole their treasure. Fearing the retribution of the Huns, he surrendered to his enemy, enabling them to enter the city (Mirković 1986, 209). Although there are no archaeological finds that would support these historical claims, we still have confirmation of the existence of an Episcopal see in *Margum* and the importance of this city in the church organisation of this region, in the middle of the 5th century.

---

[18] About early period of Christianity in the provinces of *Moesia Prima* and *Dacia Ripensis* see: Jeremić, Ilić 2018, 200–205.

Viminacium

The capital of the province of *Moesia Superior*, *Viminacium* is noted by historical sources as a significant military stronghold and the seat of the VII Claudia Legion. "On the right bank of the river Mlava, not far from the place where it flows into the Danube, an extended plateau rises, which used to be a Roman town", wrote F. Kanitz, an Austro-Hungarian researcher of antiquities, about the remains of *Viminacium*, when he came across them while travelling through Serbia in the 19th century (Kanitz 1892, 17). When the city gained the status of a *municipium* (117 AD), its territory covered a larger part of the plain in the lower course of the Mlava River, while, after acquiring the status of a colony (239 AD), *Viminacium* expanded to cover the entire Stig plain and Veliko Gradište (*Pincum*) (Popović 1967, 30). *Viminacium* was the capital of the province *Moesia Prima* and at the same time the Episcopal see. A large number of soldiers from various parts of the Empire, which were stationed in *Viminacium* as an important political and military centre, allowed the spread of numerous cults, especially those from the East, along with the official religion of the Empire (Zotović 1973, 31–33). Written data about an organised Christian community confirmed by the acts of the Council in *Serdica* from 343 AD, signed by the bishop of *Viminacium* Amantius. Along with a number of bishops from Illyricum, he was also against Arianism and its representatives, Valens from *Mursa* and Ursacius from *Singidunum* (Zeiller 1918 (rp. 1967), 234–235). From a later period, we also learn the name of another bishop, Cyriacus, who is mentioned in Athanasius' epistle from 356 AD, *Epistola contra Arianos*, which was sent to the bishops of Egypt and directed against Arianism. Cyriacus is mentioned as *Cyriacus Mysiae*. On the basis of preserved documents, it is assumed that Cyriacus could have been on the episcopal throne of the capital of *Moesia Prima* during the first half or in the middle of the 4th century (Zeiller, 1918 (rp. 1967), 148–149). In the first half of the 5th century, the bishop of *Viminacium* is mentioned in one letter to Pope Celestine I, in 424 AD (Zeiller 1918 (rp. 1967), 598). During the invasion of the Huns and later, during the 5th century, we have no information on any occurrences related to the church organisation in *Viminacium*. It is not until the 6th century that we find out from Justinian's Novella XI, from 535 AD, that the city found itself under the jurisdiction of the Archbishopric of *Iustiniana Prima*. As Procopius informs us, the renewed Episcopate was raised to the status of Metropolitanate (Popović 1967, 37, note 69).

Aquae

The Roman city of *Aquae* (near today's Prahovo, in eastern Serbia) had a long tradition and began to develop from the very first arrival of the Romans into this region, but it has not been extensively researched by archaeologists to date. It is known that the bishop of *Aquae* Vitalis was one of the participants at the Council of *Serdica* (Athanasius, *Apologia* 48, 2). The names of later bishops of the province of *Dacia Ripensis* are not known until the 6th century, when Justinian's Novella XI, from 535 AD, mentions the bishop of *Aquae,* who worked on the suppression of the heresy by Photinus, which, at the end of the 4th century, was confessed to by Bonosus (Zeiller 1918 (rp. 1967), 350). The heresy mentioned in Novella XI had roots in the teachings of Marcellus of *Ancyra* and his follower Photinus of *Sirmium*.[19] Justinian strived to finally uproot this heresy in the area of the Balkans and in his efforts, he gave a special role to the bishop of *Aquae*. From the testimonies of Procopius, we known that the territory of *Aquae* comprehended a series of *fortifications*, settlements and church buildings. Along the Danube, its territory most probably reached as far as the fortification of *Zanes*, and in the south – the area of *Naissus* (Zeiller 1918 (rp. 1967), 154–155; Mirković 1995, 207).

Romuliana

The archaeological site of *Romuliana* near Zaječar in eastern Serbia is famous for the imperial palace complex, built by Emperor Galerius at the beginning of the 4th century (Fig. 1.1).[20] The period of Late Antiquity in *Romuliana* is characterised by the first traces of Christianity. Even though it was not a settlement with the status of a city, the fortified memorial palace, named *Felix Romuliana* on the basis of an inscription discovered within the complex (Živić 2003, 23),[21] provides an interesting instance of the transformation of pagan architecture into Christian, on the example of an imperial palace as a seat of the imperial cult. Church buildings, mostly created through the adaption of chambers of the former imperial palace, bear witness to the religious aspect of the Late Antique settlement in the period from the second half of the 4th century to the 6th century (Čanak-Medić 1978, 134–149; Petković 2010, 167–199). The situation drastically changed in the 6th century: as Christianity had been the official religion of the state for two entire centuries, all the construction undertakings of the emperors Anastasius I and Justinian I regarding the restoration of old or building of new fortifications and urban centres comprehended the building of Christian temples as well.

---

[19] For the teachings of Marcellus of *Ancyra* and the bishop of *Sirmium* Photinus, see: Kartašov 1995, 64–69.

[20] There are a number of scholar works regarding the Late Antique imperial palace and later buildings built on its ruins: Čanak-Medić, M. *Gamzigrad – kasnoantička palata*, Beograd 1978; Janković, Dj. Carski dvorac, u S. Ćelić (ur.), *Gamzigrad kasnoantički carski dvorac*, Beograd 1983, 120–130; Vasić M. ed. *Felix Romuliana 50 years of archaeological excavations*, Belgrade 2006; Petković, S. Romulijana u vreme posle carske palate, u: *Felix Romuliana – Gamzigrad*, (ur.) I. Popović, Beograd 2010, 167–199; Petković, S. Late Roman Romuliana and medieval Gamzigrad from the end of 4th to the 11th centuries AD, in: *Kesythely-Fenékpuszta im Kontext spätantiker Kontinuitätsforschung zwischen Noricum und Moesia*, (hrsg.) O. Heinrich-Tamáska, Budapest... (etc.) 2011, 267–283.

[21] The inscription was discovered in 1984, in the south-western part of the palace, in the building with mosaic floors. It was carved on an archivolt made of sandstone.

Figure 1.1. Gamzigrad–*Romuliana*. General view of the palace. (Documentation of the Institute of Archaeology, Belgrade).

As we have mentioned before, there is no written data, for the time being, on the basis of which we could conclude that the fortification in *Romuliana* had the status of a city. However, considering the fact that there was a baptistery with the church, which was erected in the 6th century, some authors believe that *Romuliana* could have been an episcopal see (Janković 1983, 128–129). To date, we have no firm proof that would support this supposition. It should be mentioned, however, that it was not a rare occurrence during Late Antiquity that the act of baptism be performed in smaller rural churches, thus, we could assume that this was also one such church (Ilić 2008, 240). In any case, churches discovered in *Romuliana* so far that have been dated into the period from the 4th to the 6th century – two of them had a baptistery – indicate the intense Christianisation process of the local population of the province of *Dacia Ripensis* in this period.

2

Sacral Architecture

2.1. Churches

The overview of Early Christian monuments in the territory of the provinces of *Moesia Prima* and *Dacia Ripensis* provides a picture of how they were created and how they developed, from the very beginning up to the times when the entire ecclesiastic organisation fell under the force of the Avar–Slav invasion at the beginning of the 7th century. The presence of Christian communities has been archaeologically confirmed at numerous sites in the territory of Northern Illyricum in the period from the 4th up to the beginning of the 7th century.

Christian ecclesiastic building activities have been archaeologically documented in larger urban centres, but also in fortresses along the Danube Limes (Map 2.1). They reached their full pinnacle only from the reign of Anastasius (491–518), but especially so under Justinian I (527–565). Among the most important cities of the *Moesia Prima* province are two provincial metropolises – *Singidunum*

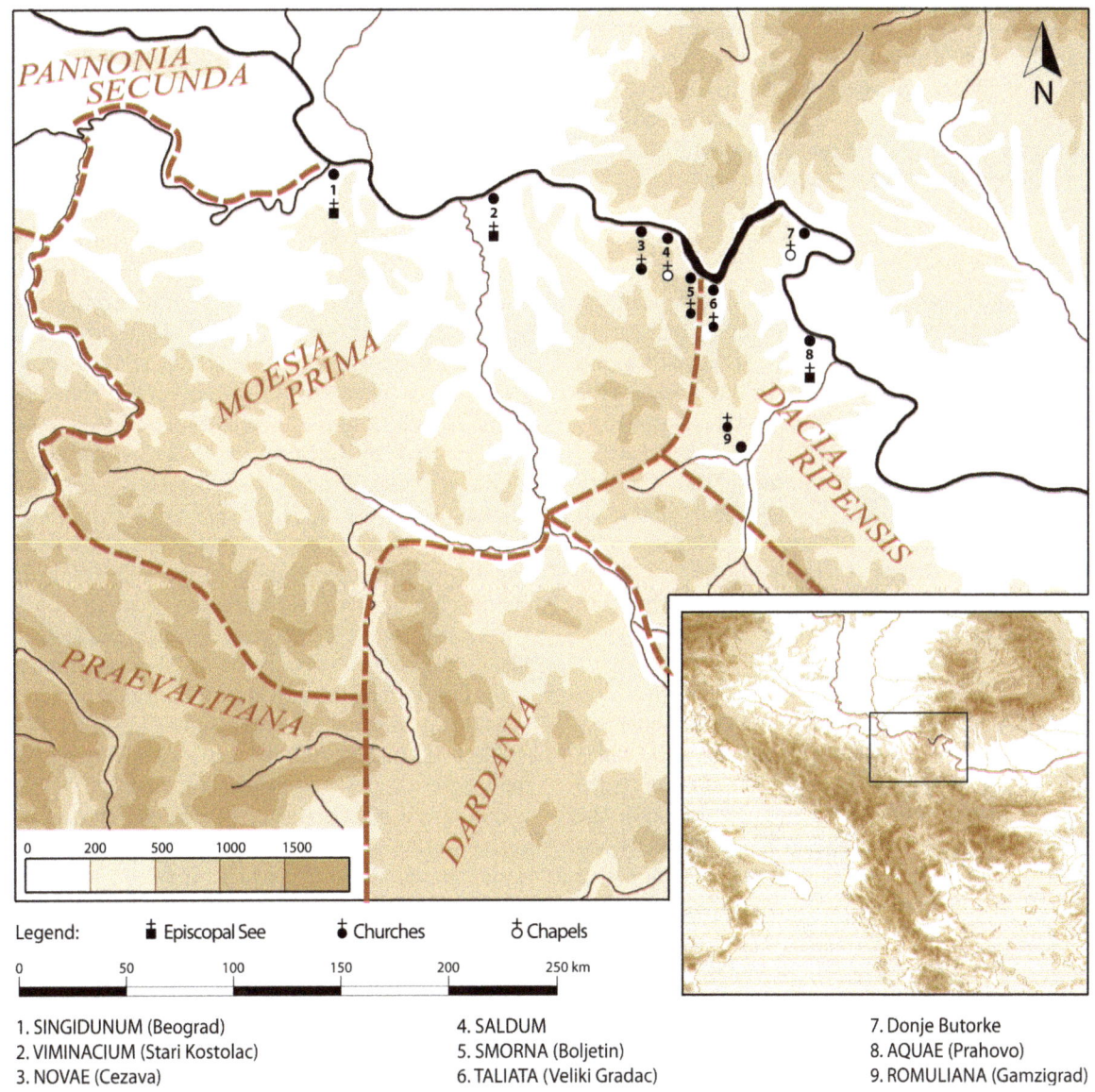

Legend: ♁ Episcopal See   • Churches   ○ Chapels

1. SINGIDUNUM (Beograd)
2. VIMINACIUM (Stari Kostolac)
3. NOVAE (Cezava)
4. SALDUM
5. SMORNA (Boljetin)
6. TALIATA (Veliki Gradac)
7. Donje Butorke
8. AQUAE (Prahovo)
9. ROMULIANA (Gamzigrad)

Map 2.1. The Early Christian sites with sacral architecture in the provinces of *Moesia Prima* and *Dacia Ripensis*.

and *Viminacium*, in which relatively modest traces of the presence of Christian communities during Late Antiquity have been found, although they were episcopal sees since the 4th century.

No traces of sacral architecture have yet been discovered in *Singidunum*. There are thick layers of modern, Ottoman and medieval settlements in the area where early Christian churches could be expected.[22] Among today's researchers of Belgrade Fortress, there is an opinion about the possible location of an early Christian church in the area of the interior of the legionary fort of *Singidunum*, but foundations of a structure that could be potentially identified as an early Christian basilica have not been found yet.

Even though the research activities in *Viminacium* have been ongoing for over a century, the area of the legionary camp and the civilian urban city have been researched to a lesser extent compared to the necropolises of *Viminacium* (Fig. 2.1). Some researchers have assumed that luxurious family tombs had been used as places intended for the Christian cult as well (Zotović 1986, 41–60; Zotović 1994, 60–63). It would seem, however, that they could have been used merely for paying homage and for cult rites dedicated to individuals buried in those tombs, but not for a wider use, for which church buildings were used instead.

Romuliana (Gamzigrad)

In Late Antique *Romuliana* the oldest church building, basilica I, was erected in the southern access halls of the imperial palace (Fig. 2.2). The three-nave basilica was built into one of the chambers of the imperial palace. The length of the lateral naves was 24 m, and the central nave with the apse 27.4 m. A part of the stylobate above the foundations, as well as the pedestals for columns or pillars were built with bricks, while the foundations were made of stone. Basilica I was built at the end of the 4th or the beginning of the 5th century (Čanak-Medić 1978, 130, fig. 121). It most probably remained in use all the way until the restoration or the building of a new church in the same place.

A new three-nave basilica II was constructed above the older basilica I, with an apse on the eastern side, which was trapezoidal on the outside and semi-circular on the inside, with dimensions of 31.5 m x 27 m (Fig. 2.3). The altar space, which was pentagonal on the outside, consisted of a rectangular part (5.7 m x 3.3 m) and an apse with a depth of 3.2 m. The preserved northern wall of the palace chamber was used for the foundations of the northern wall, while the foundations of the main nave were placed along the inner side of the older basilica I. Only the foundations of this church were preserved, constructed from different stone types bound with lime mortar. A tetraconchal baptistery was built along the southern nave of the basilica. According to the pottery finds from the 6th century, mostly stove tiles, the basilica was dated into the 6th century, most probably in the time of Justinian's restoration of *Romuliana* (Čanak-Medić 1978, 138, fig. 124).

The opulent Late Antique imperial palace suffered the fate of many Roman cities during the time of the Great Migration. In parallel with the erection of simple living spaces in destroyed parts of the palace, a single-nave church was also built, created by adapting one of the chambers of the Late Antique palace, most probably at the beginning of the 5th century (Petković 2010b, 197). Somewhat later, at the end of the 5th or the beginning of the 6th century, a smaller sacral building with a semi-circular apse facing east, most likely a baptistery, was constructed using the dry stone technique (Fig. 2.4), (Janković 1983, 122, fig. 91).[23] The piscine of a cruciform shape, was encompassed by a wall made from bricks and lime mortar, placed west of the apse, above the floor. In the area where the palace once was, to the west of the imperial *thermae*, another three-nave basilica was erected in the 6th century, which has been partially researched (Petković, 2010b, 197).

Churches on the Middle Danube Limes

The churches of the Roman military fortifications in the regions of the Middle Danube Limes, which was one of the best fortified borders in the central Balkans, with numerous troops stationed in them, deserve special attention. Even though the majority of settlements and fortifications were destroyed during the Hun invasion in the middle of the 5th century, a considerable number were restored by Justinian's fortification activity in the Balkans, which Procopius described in detail in his famous work (Procop. *De Aedif.* IV, 5–6, p. 267–271). The interconnection between the Middle Danube Limes and the church organisation in the Balkans in the 6th century has not received sufficient attention as yet. The manuscript *De aedificiis* provides firm evidence that in the middle of the 6th century the fortification of the border at the Danube and the provinces in the inner parts reached a level that had not been registered before in the Balkans. Aside from that, during the first half of the 6th century, the weakened city government was replaced by bishops, whose power extended even beyond the borders of their episcopacies. For example, the bishop of the city of *Aquae*, mentioned in *Novella* XI from 535 AD, to whose authority both the city and the near-by fortifications (*castella*) were subjected, because he was expected to "expel the crime of the Bonociaci (heretics) from that city and territory and bring (the people) (back) to the orthodox faith" (*Nov.* XI).

---

[22] Excavations at Belgrade Fortress have been conducted for several decades by the Archaeological Institute in Belgrade, but with the exception of rare objects of early Christian characteristics, such as the so-called Jonah's sarcophagus, which will be discussed in more detail in the next chapter, remains of church architecture have not been identified.

[23] According to one of the researchers of the site of *Romuliana*, S. Petković, a detailed architectonical analysis and a chronological delineation of building phases of churches in the site of Gamzigrad (*Romuliana*) hasn't been performed yet, therefore, the function and the dating of these two buildings isn't completely reliable.

Figure 2.1. Kostolac–*Viminacium*. Plan of the city and legionary camp. (Documentation of the Institute of Archaeology, Belgrade).

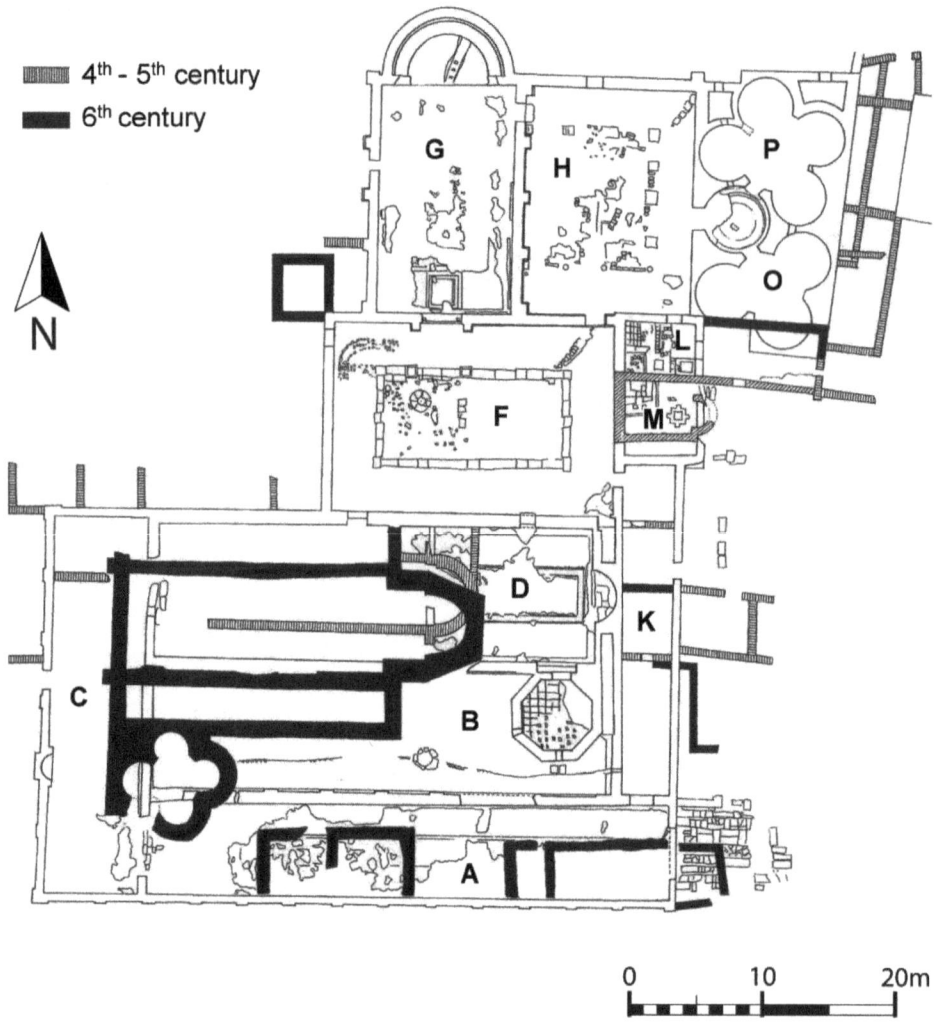

Figure 2.2. Gamzigrad–*Romuliana*. Basilica I and basilica II in the southern part of the Late Antique palace. (Documentation of the Institute of Archaeology, Belgrade).

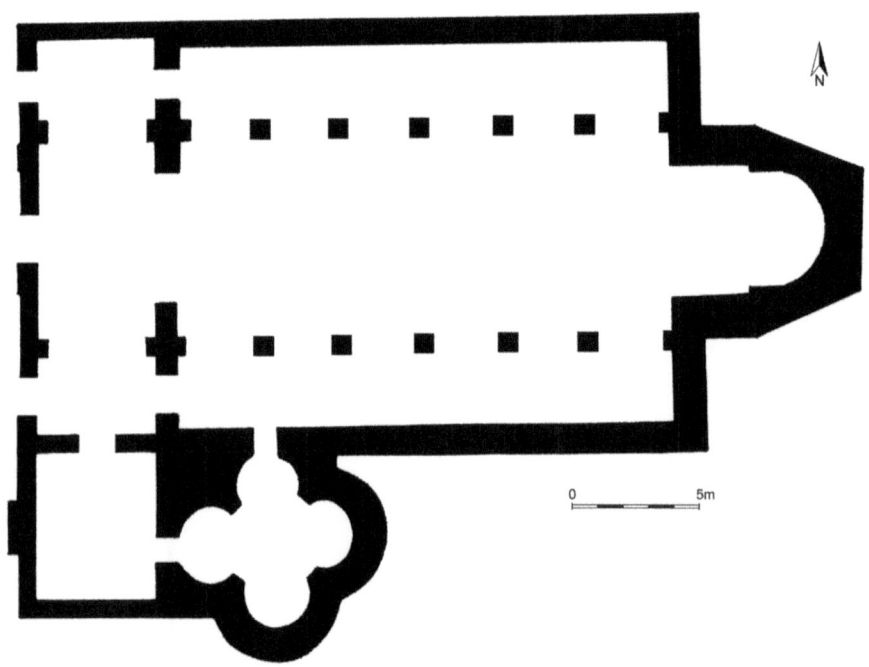

Figure 2.3. Gamzigrad–*Romuliana*. Plan of the three-nave basilica II. (Documentation of the Institute of Archaeology, Belgrade).

Sacral Architecture

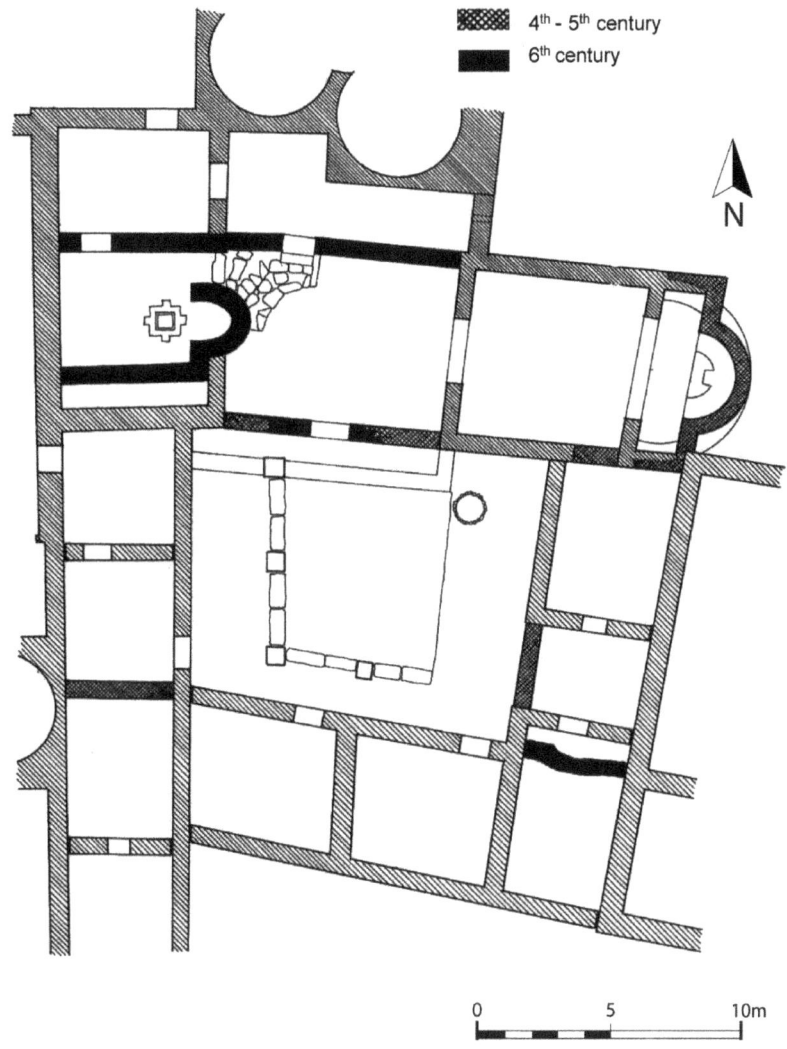

Figure 2.4. Gamzigrad–*Romuliana*. Plan of the church and baptistery in the eastern part of the Late Antique palace. (Documentation of the Institute of Archaeology, Belgrade).

Several decades long rescue archaeological excavations at the Iron Gates Limes brought to light a large number of remains of both military and civilian architecture, but also different archaeological findings. During Late Antiquity, remains of Early Christian sacral buildings, and parts of church inventories, as well as items of profane use with clear Christian traits have been registered along the entire part of the Limes belonging to the provinces of *Moesia Prima* and *Dacia Ripensis*. In this part of the Limes, episcopal seats have not been confirmed. The church buildings were primarily used for the military occupants of the fortification. The existence of baptisteries in churches within fortifications, such as *Smorna* or *Taliata*, indicates that the baptismal sacrament was being performed among the soldiers. The early Byzantine fortifications along the Iron Gates Limes were small, with areas of often no more than half a hectare, and they could not have been serviced by more than 300 to 400 soldiers. In any case, since there were no traces of civilian life, the baptisteries had to have been intended first and foremost for the military. Whether baptisms were performed in them for the population that lived in the immediate vicinity, for now we cannot offer a reliable answer. All these numerous material remains indicate the presence of an already well organised Christian community among the soldiers of the Roman Empire, but also the civilian population in this region. Remains of Early Christian ecclesiastic architecture registered within several fortifications chronologically belong to the early Byzantine period, i.e., the reign of Justinian I, who strived to fortify the border along the Danube Limes, but also to strengthen the influence of the Early Christian church in the territory of the entire Northern Illyricum. Traces of early Byzantine church buildings have been registered within the fortifications at *Novae* (Čezava), *Smorna* (Boljetin) and *Taliata* (Veliki Gradac) (Map 2.1).[24]

The Roman system of building military encampments endured certain changes during the times of Justinian I. The restored Roman fortifications and the newly built Byzantine ones included new elements as well. Among other things, certain fortifications now included a Christian church as a very important religious building.

[24] A short overview of Early Christian churches and chapels at the Iron Gates Limes, see: G. Jeremić, O. Ilić 2018, 205–224.

The main military centre of the Iron Gates Limes was *Taliata* (Veliki Gradac), which played, in terms of the military system, the primary role among all other fortifications in this part of the Limes. Thus, *Taliata* also became the main ecclesiastic centre for this area. Within the fortification, a single-nave church was built, with all the elements necessary to perform the ceremonies of the Christian cult. The baptistery with a piscina under the canopy indicates its rank and importance in an ecclesiastic sense. In *Smorna*, as one of the larger fort along the Iron Gates Limes, a single-nave church was built, with a narthex, katechoumenon and probably a baptistery.

Novae (Čezava)

At the confluence of the river Čezava and the Danube, the castrum *Novae* was built. From here, the road along the Danube began, on which a series of fortifications and military stations lined up one after the other. Traces of early Christianity are not so numerous in this area, but the remains of church architecture on several sites have been preserved, mainly from the period of Justinian's construction activity and the restoration of the Danube Limes, which was destroyed in the middle of the 5th century during the Hun invasion. In the north-western part of the fortification of *Novae* there are the foundation remains of two churches constructed one above the other, the later of which has been completely investigated (Vasić 1984, 103, fig. 9). Foundations of two single-nave churches have been discovered, which had been built one on top of the other. The church that was erected later is somewhat smaller (Fig. 2.5). It consists of a rectangular naos with a narthex in front, with added lateral annexes, while the semi-circular apse is to the east (length: 22 m, apse depth: 2 m) (Vasić 1984, T. VI 1, 2). Along the outer wall of the apse of the older church, counterforts were registered (Vasić 1984, T. VI 3). Along the inner wall of the apse of the more recent church, remains of a semi-circular bench (*subselium*) were preserved (Fig. 2.6). There are annexes on both sides of the narthex, the southern one ending with an apse. This room probably had a cult function (*chonephtirion*), since a marble *mortarium* was found in it (Vasić 1995, 49). There are partially preserved remains of a mortar floor. Both churches are indicative of the time of Justinian I, after 543/4 AD, although their stratigraphy cannot be determined with precision, nor can they be dated on the basis of the material found. The most recent coins discovered in the fort of Čezava belong to Mauricius, 593/594 AD, indicating the time when the fortification was destroyed and abandoned (Vasić 1984, 102).

Smorna (Boljetin)

The castrum in Boljetin, which was identified as the Roman *Smorna*, is one of the better preserved fort on the Danube Limes. The fortification had a long development due to its strategic position. We find traces from the very arrival of the Romans from the 1st century to the early Byzantine fortification in the 6th century (Figs. 2.7, 2.8), (Zotović 1984, 211–229). During the early Byzantine renovation of the fortress in the 6th century (third construction period), a single-nave church was built. It has an east-west

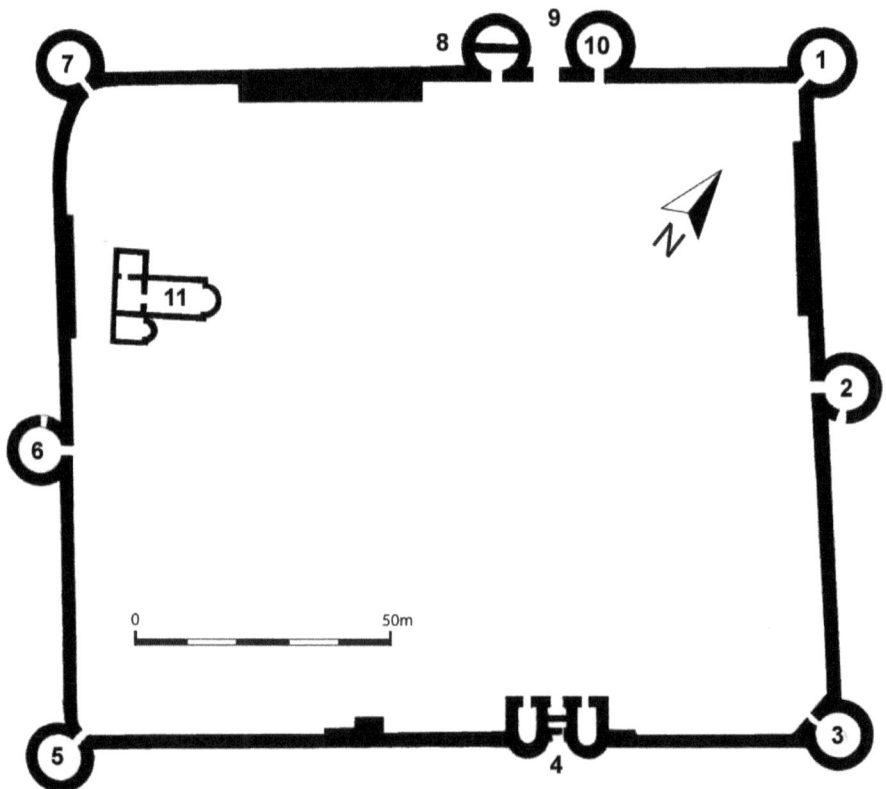

Figure 2.5. Čezava–*Novae*. Plan of the fortification and the church. (After: Vasić 1984, 103, Figure 9).

Figure 2.6. Čezava–*Novae*. The church from the 6th century, detail. (Documentation of the Institute of Archaeology, Belgrade).

Figure 2.7. Boljetin–*Smorna*. General view of the fortification and the church. (Documentation of the Institute of Archaeology, Belgrade).

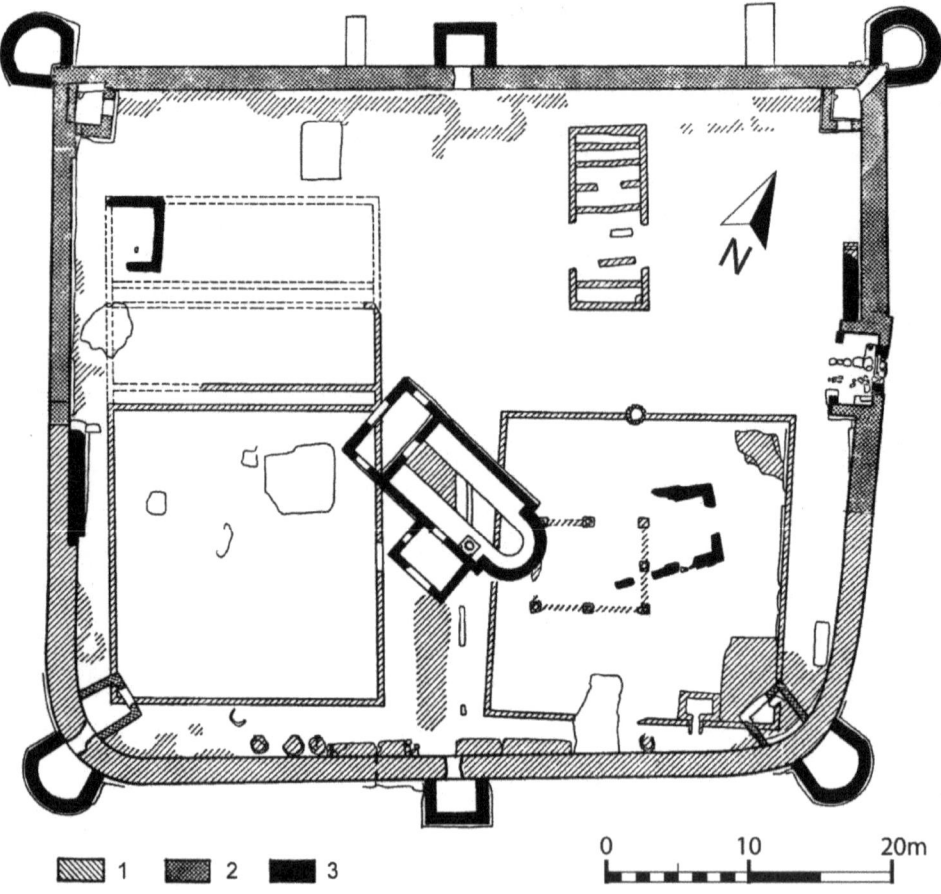

Figure 2.8. Boljetin–*Smorna*. Plan of the fortification and the church. (After: Zotović 1984, 213, Figure 2).

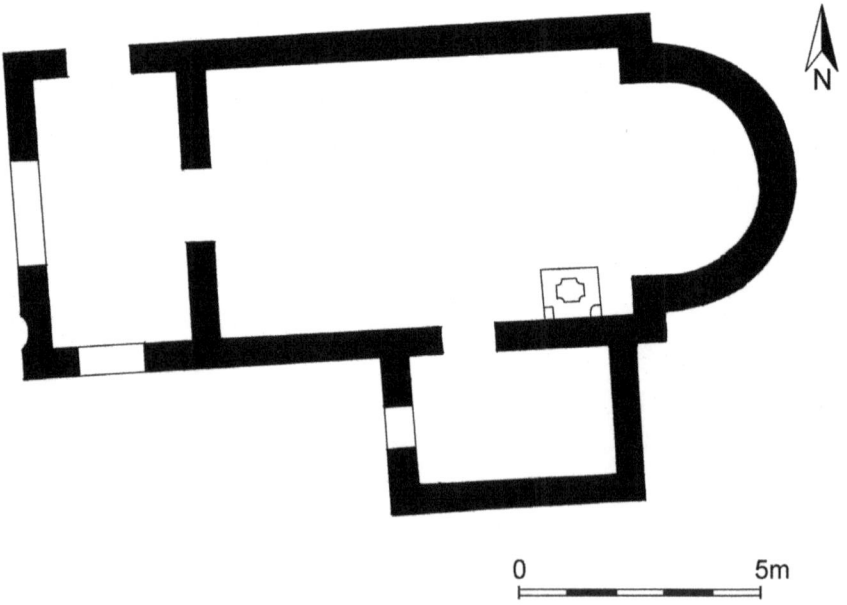

Figure 2.9. Boljetin–*Smorna*. Early Christian church, ground plan. (Documentation of the Institute of Archaeology, Belgrade).

orientation (dimensions of 15 x 5.5 m). The church consists of a rectangular naos, a semi-circular apse in the east and a narthex on the western side, which was added at a later point (Fig. 2.9). On the inner side of the apse wall there is a part preserved in the form of a bench, probably remains of seats (*subsellium*) (Fig. 2.10a). Along the southern wall of the naos, close to the altar area, a rectangular annex was added, with a separate entrance from the outside, but it was also connected to the naos. On the inner side of the southern wall of the naos, opposite this annex, right next

Sacral Architecture

Figure 2.10. a-b. Boljetin–*Smorna*. a) apse with the baptistery; b) detail of the baptistery. (Documentation of the Institute of Archaeology, Belgrade).

to the apse, the remains were discovered of a cross-shaped baptistery. It was built from bricks joined with mortar, and plastered with two layers of mortar, with a piscine for baptisms (Fig. 2.10b), (Ilić 2006, 226). The outside of the piscine was in the shape of a cross. It was built of brick, and covered with two layers of lime mortar. The purpose of the annex on the southern side could be described as a catechumenon, given the installation for baptism positioned along the southern wall of the naos. This would correspond fully with the liturgical rites of that time because only baptised neophytes had the right to attend the liturgy, standing in the naos of the church (Popović 1995 (rp. 1912), 430–432). It is evident that the church and baptistery were primarily for the use of the military inhabitants of the fortification. All parts of the church were built using the same technique, with alternations of rubble and broken stone and bricks. The substructure of the apse floor, the naos and the annex on the southern side consisted of regularly placed pebbles. They were covered in mortar, with a thick layer of mortar on top of it, in which bricks were laid, which negatives were registered during the excavation (Zotović 1984, 223).

The church in *Smorna* dates back to the last phase of the fortification. Inside the church, not far from the altar, coins of Justinus I, Justinian I, Justinus II and Mauricius were discovered, according to which one may draw the conclusion that the castrum was abandoned in the last years of the 6th century. Many of the buildings within the fortress, bear the marks of a large scale fire, which may well coincide with the invasion by the Avars and the Slavs at the end of the 6th century (Zotović 1984, 224).

Taliata **(Veliki Gradac)**

The fortress of *Taliata* at the Veliki Gradac site, lay on the border of the province of *Moesia Prima* and *Dacia Ripensis*. It was built on the important Danube road that led to the east from *Singidunum* via *Viminacium*, representing an important defensive point against enemy incursions from the territory of *Dacia*.

Traces of this fortification were noticed by Marsigli, and later by Kanitz (Marsigli 1726, 19; Kanitz 1892, 35). The first ramparts of the fortress were built in the 1st century AD (Popović 1984, 266). In the time of Justinian I, the ramparts were renovated with circular towers on the corners, in accordance with the then fortification system (Fig. 2.11). The church in the fortification of *Taliata* was constructed within the ramparts of the fort, along the tower of the western rampart. It is oriented along an east–west axis, with a small deviation due to the layout of the western rampart of the fortification (Fig. 2.12). The dimensions of the naos are 9.5 x 5.9 m, with a semi-circular altar apse 3.4 m deep. A rectangular narthex is in the west, dimensions 5.8 x 4.3 m. On the southern side of the church, near the apse, an annex was subsequently built, with the entrance on the west. The church was built of bricks, with mortar joints (*opus mixtum*) (Popović 1984, 276, fig. 6). There was no communication between the naos and the annex, so we can suppose that this area did not serve as a catechumenon, as it did in the previously mentioned example in *Smorna*. The area of the former gate was walled up in the 6th century, and the tower was transformed into a baptistery (Popović 1984, 276, T. VII, 3). It is attached to the narthex, measuring 8.2 x 3.5 m. The baptismal piscine was placed in the southern section of the tower. It was made of bricks joined with mortar (Fig. 2.13). The piscine was of an irregular circular shape. At its corners were four columns, probably supports for a baldachin (Ilić 2006, 226–227). One descended into it by means of steps on the western side and emerged by another set of steps on the eastern side, after the baptismal ceremony was completed. The church in the castrum of *Taliata* was built using the *opus mixtum* technique, with brick walls. Researchers discovered two phases of reconstruction, based on differences in the floors and the finishing of the church walls (Popović 1984, 276, fig. 6).

According to researchers, the floors and walls of the church indicate the existence of two building phases (Popović 1984, 276). As with other church buildings along the Danube Limes, the manner of construction, as well as the archaeological finds (follis of Justinus II), indicate that

Late Antiquity and Early Christianity in the Roman Provinces of Moesia Prima and Dacia Ripensis

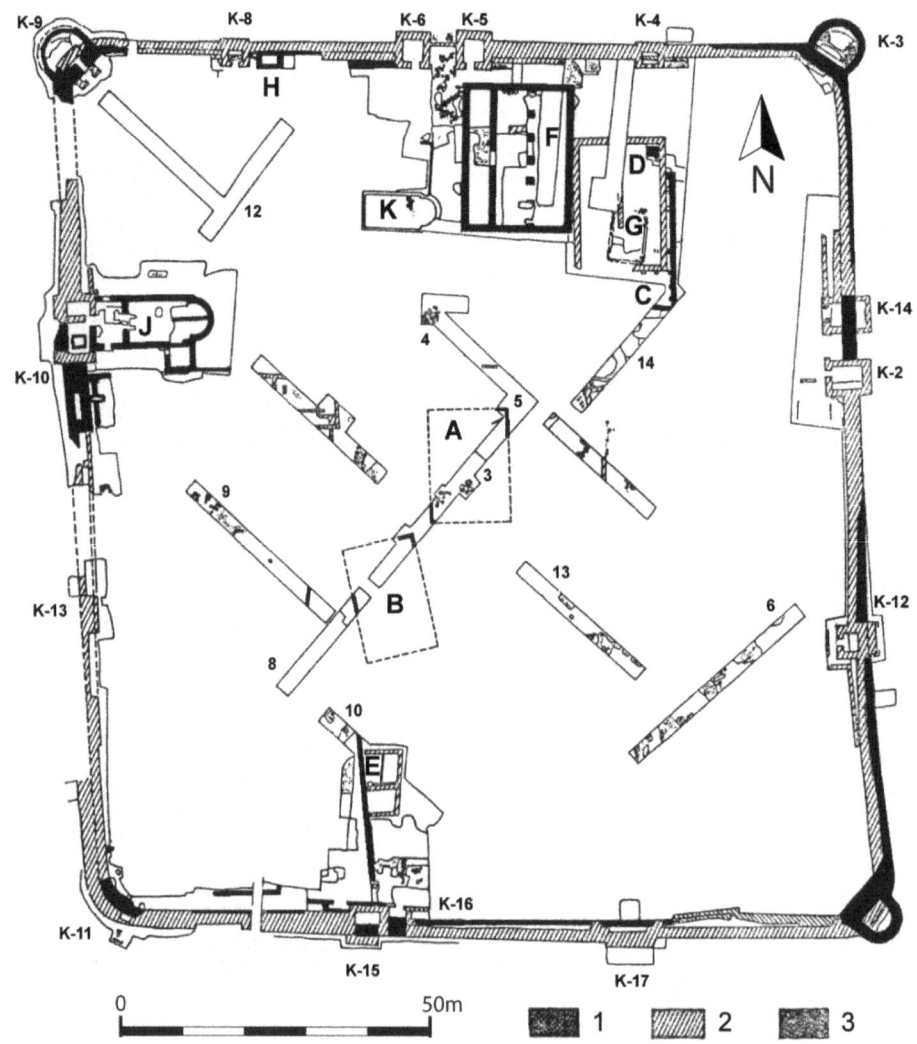

Figure 2.11. Donji Milanovac–*Taliata*. Plan of the fortification and the church. (After: Popović 1984, 266, Figure 1).

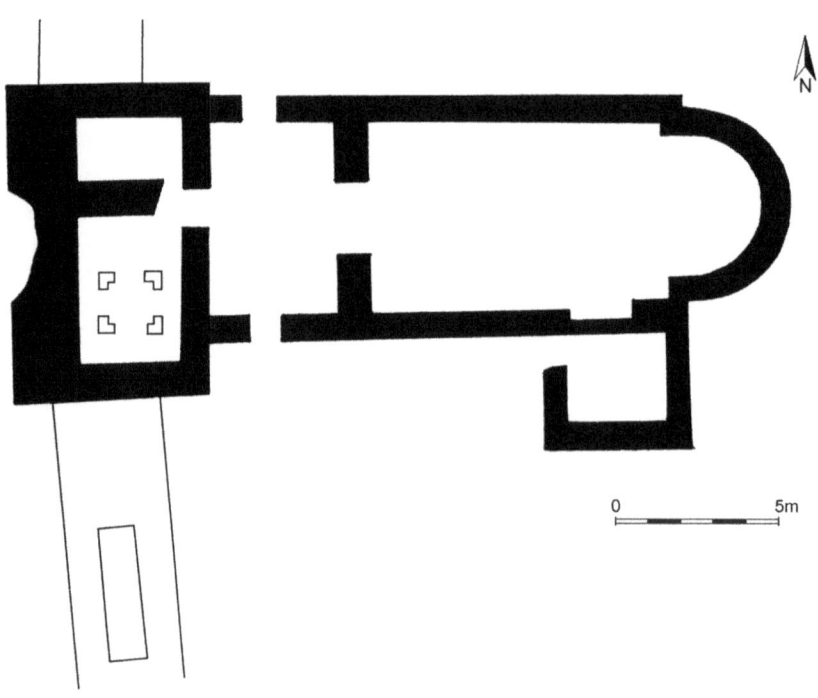

Figure 2.12. Donji Milanovac–*Taliata*. Early Christian church, ground plan. (Documentation of the Institute of Archaeology, Belgrade).

Figure 2.13. Donji Milanovac–*Taliata*. A baptistery erected inside the previous tower, detail. (Documentation of the Institute of Archaeology, Belgrade).

the church was erected during the early Byzantine period, in the time of Justinian's renovation. The fortification at *Taliata* was destroyed during Avar-Slav attacks on the Empire in 595/596 AD (Popović 1984, 280).

2.2. Chapels

Within the Limes fortifications, in the area where the erection of a church itself was difficult due to the configuration of the terrain and the narrowed space, small chapels were formed for the needs of the fort's cohort, the so-called military chapels in one of the towers whose shape was modified and adapted to the needs of the Christian rite.

Saldum

Not far from the aforementioned castrum of *Novae* (Čezava), there is the Roman fortress of Saldum, on the site of Gradac, a Late Antique and early Byzantine fort that was used for the accommodation of auxiliary troops (Petrović 1984, 128–134). The fortification of *Saldum* was restored during the great restoration of the Danube Limes in the 6th century, during the reign of Justinian I. The fort is rectangular, with three round towers on the corners, while the fourth tower, on the north-eastern corner, had a rectangular foundation, with an apse on the eastern side (Fig. 2.14) (Jeremić 2009, 47; Jeremić, Ilić 2018, 220, figs. 18, 19).

The inside of this tower was significantly destroyed by erosion, hence, there is no archaeological material that could allow us to reliably determine its function (Fig. 2.15). However, its position and orientation indicate that it could have been a building used in the Christian cult, a chapel intended mainly for Roman soldiers stationed on the Danube Limes.

Donje Butorke

The fortification at the site of Donje Butorke, in the vicinity of the large *castrum Diana* is of a roughly square shape (Cermanović-Kuzmanović 1979, 129). During Justinian's restoration of the Danube Limes, round towers were built on the corners (Cermanović-Kuzmanović 1979, 133: Jeremić, Ilić 2018, 221, figs. 21, 22). Approximately in the middle of the south-eastern rampart, a rectangular tower was built, ending with an apse (5.5 x 3.2 m) (Fig. 2.16). According to its shape, it is very similar to the one already mentioned from *Saldum* and, hence, it can be assumed that it had the same purpose, that is to say, that it served as a chapel for the military crew of the fortification during the 6th century (Jeremić 2009, 47).

Late Antiquity and Early Christianity in the Roman Provinces of Moesia Prima and Dacia Ripensis

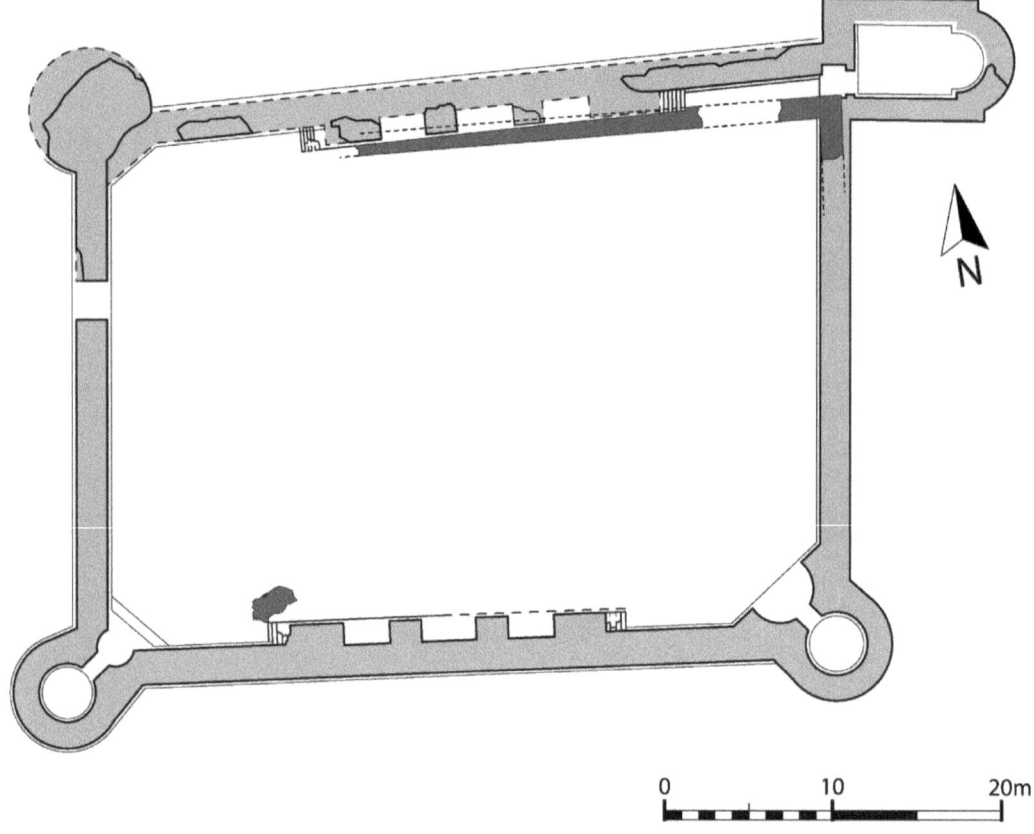

Figure 2.14. Saldum. Plan of the fortification with a tower used as a chapel. (After: Jeremić 2009, 33, Figure 19).

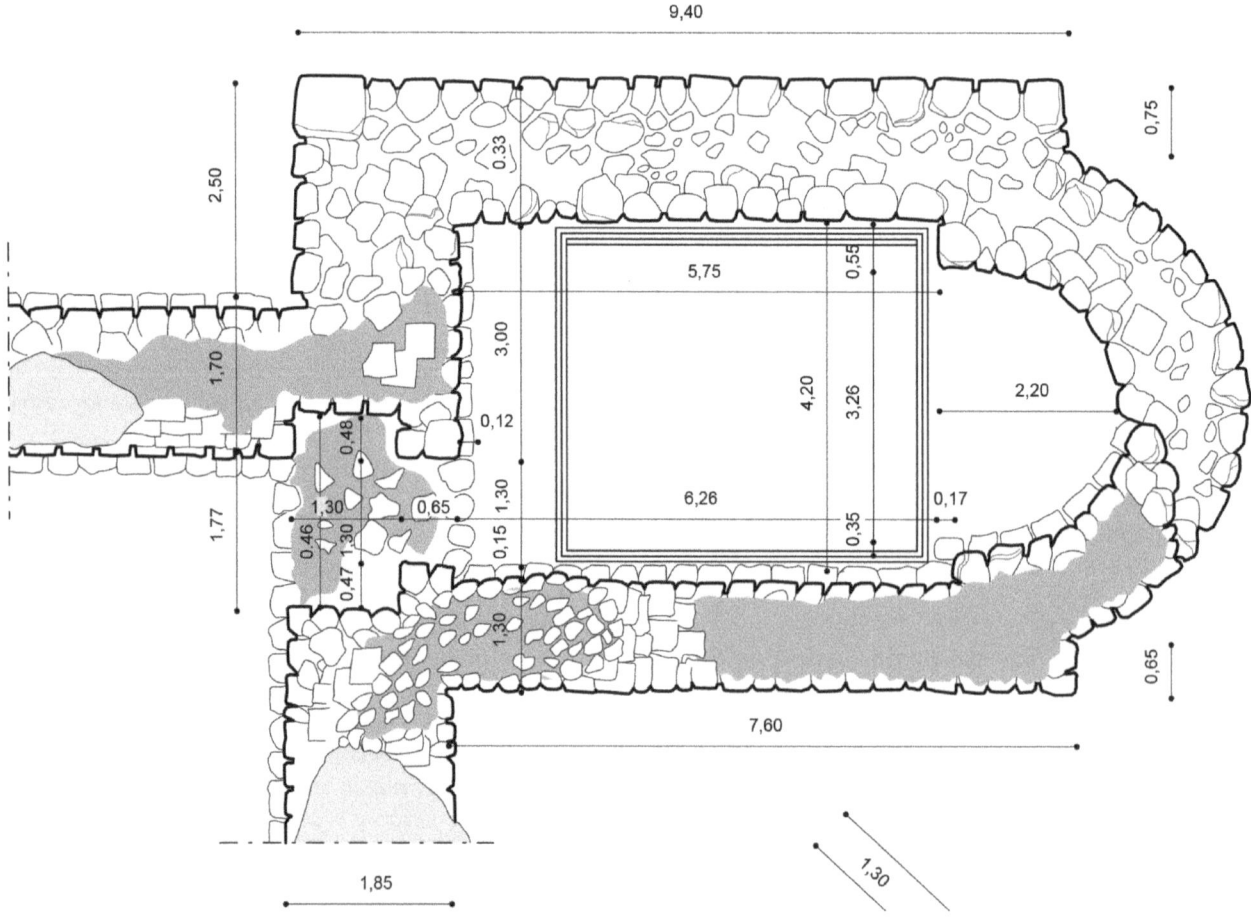

Figure 2.15. Saldum. NE tower – chapel, ground plan. (After: Jeremić 2009, 41, Figure 28a).

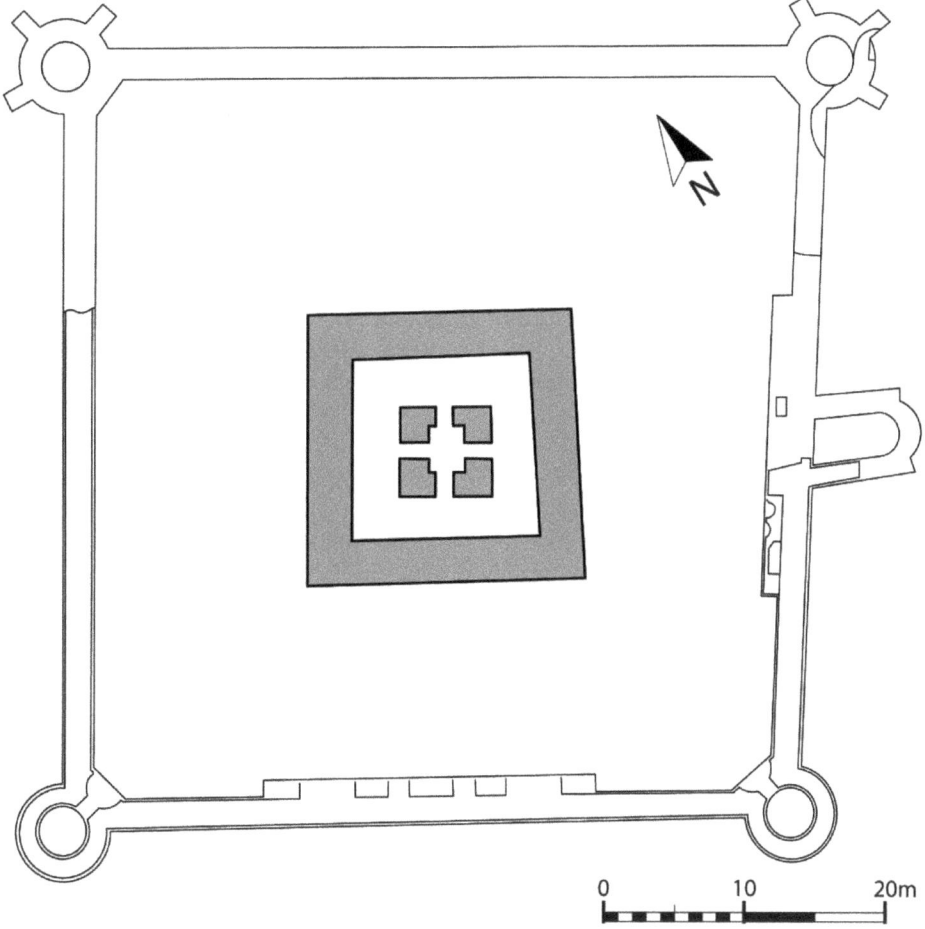

Figure 2.16. Donje Butorke. Plan of the fortification with a tower used as a chapel. (After: Jeremić 2007, 311, Figure 3, 4).

2.3. Baptisteries

The early Christian baptisteries, their position and appearance, shed light in their own way not only on the place and significance of the church building where they were or to which they were attached, they also reveal the method of baptism itself and the specific local features that were often reflected in their spatial articulation. Adapted to the most essential needs of the rite of baptism, they were simple rooms, frequently with an irregular ground plan and sometimes with no inside decorative elements at all. Though exhibiting great diversity in their design, in most cases, they constituted part of the church building itself; however, in a few cases they occurred as separate buildings. In the period of Late Antiquity, they were not unique, but were a common feature throughout the broader Mediterranean region.

At the beginning of the 4th century, the Christians, as an already sizeable and influential societal force within the Roman Empire, were granted freedom to profess their faith. The emperor Theodosius I proclaims Christianity to be the main religion in the Roman Empire and issued the edict *Cunctos populous* (Šukunda 2017, 316–319). This event brought changes not only to its internal administrative organisation but also in the domain of the architectural and artistic canons for sacral buildings. At that time, architectonic forms were still modest, but they would become more elaborate as the political and economic importance of the church grew. During this period, large urban centres acquired their first basilicas, as did the smaller towns and fortresses. Initially, sacral buildings were erected that needed to be equipped with installations that would be used in the increasing mass baptisms of catechumens in the episcopal centres, and later in smaller urban agglomerations, as in the rural areas. The organisation of the Church corresponded to the administrative organisation of the provinces, so that the major cities also became episcopal seats (Popović 1995, 29). The rise and fall of ecclesiastical life in the Balkans, and thus in the Danube provinces of *Moesia Prima* and *Dacia Ripensis*, in the period of Late Antiquity, was closely bound to the changing political circumstances the provinces of the Illyrian prefecture were exposed to.

Romuliana (Gamzigrad)

In parallel with the erection of simple living spaces in destroyed parts of the the Late Antique palace, most probably at the beginning of the 5th century, a single-nave church was built, by adapting one of the chambers of the palace (Fig. 2.4), (Petković 2010b, 197). A small sacral building with a semi-circular apse facing east was later built next to this church, during the 5th or the beginning of the 6th century, most likely a baptistery (Janković 1983, 122). The piscine, of a cruciform shape, was encompassed by a wall made from bricks and lime mortar, placed west of the apse, above the floor. The central part of the piscine had a rectangular base, lined with marble slabs, the dimensions of which were 0.56 x 0.52 m. The preserved part of the bottom of the piscine was at a depth of 0.74 m. The opening in the bottom of the piscine was connected to a drain. According to the level of the steps leading into the baptistery, it is assumed that the upper level of the piscine (that is, its edge or frame) was elevated several dozen centimetres above the floor (Čanak-Medić 1978, 135). Given the small dimensions of the piscine, it may have served for baptising children, although one should not exclude the likelihood of it having been used for adults as well. However, in that case, the baptisms would have been possible only by means of partial immersion in the water, with additional aspersion. In the north-western quarter of the *Romuliana* complex of the Late Antique palace, another baptistery was discovered (Fig. 2.3). It was a structure with a quadrifoliate base, constructed as part of a large, triple-nave basilica in the 6th century (Čanak-Medić 1978, 138, sl. 124).[25]

Smorna (Boljetin)

In one of the better preserved fortification on the Danube Limes at *Smorna* (Boljetin), a single-nave church was erected in the central part of the fort, which had a semi-circular apse on the eastern and a narthex on the western side (Fig. 2.9). On the inner side of the southern wall of the naos, opposite this annex, the remains of a baptistery with a piscine for baptisms were discovered, with dimensions of 1.20 x 1.00 m (Fig. 2.10a-b). The outside of the piscine was in the shape of a cross. It was built of brick and covered with two layers of lime mortar. The purpose of the annex on the southern side could be described as a catechumenon, given the installation for baptisms positioned along the southern wall of the naos. This would correspond fully with the liturgical rules of that time, because only baptised neophytes had the right to attend the liturgy, standing in the naos of the church (Popović 1912 (rp. 1995), 430–432).

A similar example was recorded on the southern side of a single-nave church building at the Tsébélda site, on the eastern shores of the Black Sea (Khroushkova 1981, 17, fig. 2). In contrast to the *Smorna* baptistry, where the piscine was placed in the eastern part of the church naos, at the Tsébélda site, the baptismal section was installed in the south-western annex, located next to the room that extended along the southern nave of the church towards the altar area, which probably functioned as a catechumenon, and both rooms were linked to the naos of the church. The church with a baptistery in the fort of *Smorna* (Boljetin) dates back to the last phase of fortification the early Byzantine period. Inside it, not far from the altar, coins of Justinus I, Justinian I, Justinus II and Mauricius indicate the date of its destruction (Zotović 1984, 223–224).

Taliata (Veliki Gradac)

Inside another fortress on the Danubian Limes, *Taliata* (Veliki Gradac), which lay on the border of the provinces of *Moesia Prima* and *Dacia Ripensis*, there was a church, which was similar to the previously mentioned example, with a semi-circular altar apse facing eastwards, a narthex on the left side and an annex added later along the southern wall of the naos, close to the apse section, with an opening for the entrance in its western wall (Fig. 2.12). There was no communicating link between the naos and the annex, so we can suppose that this area did not serve as a catechumenon, as it did in the previously mentioned examples.

The area of the former gate was walled up in the 6th century, and one of the towers of the fortress transformed into a baptistery, with dimensions of 8.20 x 3.50 m. The baptismal piscine was placed in the southern section of the tower (Fig. 2.13). It was made of bricks joined with mortar. The piscine was of an irregular circular shape, it was built-in and sunken in the space. One descended into it by means of steps on the western side and emerged by another set of steps on the eastern side, after the baptismal ceremony was completed. At its corners were four columns, probably supports for a baldachin (Popović 1984, 276). According to the archaeological finds, it has been concluded that the church and the baptistery were built during the time of Justinian's renovation of the *Taliata* fort. The find of a follis of Justinus I between the flooring of the naos of the church (where two stages of construction were evidenced) confirm the early Byzantine attribution of the church. Over time, the fort degraded and low quality reconstructions were performed on some of the buildings inside it, as evidenced in the church (Popović 1984, 280). This fortified settlement in *Taliata* was destroyed during Avar attacks at the and of the 6th century (Popović 1984, 280).[26]

In the area of the Danube Valley provinces of *Moesia Prima* and *Dacia Ripensis*, baptisteries represent constructions incorporated into the church building itself. Among them, we can distinguish two types on the basis of their position in regard to the church to which they belong: baptisteries erected directly in the western part of the church, along the narthex (*Taliata*, single-nave church in *Romuliana*) and baptisteries placed in the actual naos of the church, predominantly in the eastern part, closer to the altar (*Smorna*). A baptistery in a quatrefoil shape, located along

---

[25] According to the researchers of this church, its construction was never completed, so we can't say more about this baptistery.

[26] In the Middle Ages, on the area of church, a medieval necropolis, structured in rows, was formed in 11th and 12th century, with a smaller single-nave church in the vicinity of the northern gate of the early Byzantine fortification.

the southern nave of a large three-nave basilica from the 6th century, in *Romuliana*, should be especially singled out.

Piscinae appear in various shapes, most commonly in the form of a cross. Aside from the cruciform ones, there are also round *piscinae*. The approach to the *piscina* was most often resolved with a double-staircase construction. In our region, the staircase was preserved in the baptistery of the church in *Taliata*, and in the single-nave church in *Romuliana*. The dimensions of *piscinae* can differ greatly, indicating that in the period from the 4th to the end of the 6th century, two different rites of baptism functioned in parallel – *immersion* and *aspersion*.

In most cases, baptisteries from the wider region of the Balkans are characterised by simple architectonical solutions and modest, or completely absent, decorative elements, which is not surprising, considering the fact that they were mostly built in smaller rural locations or within military forts along the Danube Limes. An exception is the richly decorated baptistery within the episcopal basilica in *Iustiniana Prima* (province of *Dacia Mediterranea*), which is illustrated by the finds of luxuriant composite capitals, marble slabs, mosaics of glass paste, as well as fragments of frescoes (Ilić 2008, 223–243). The presence of baptisteries in smaller churches built along the Danube Limes indicates the existence of a large number of catechumens, which led to the transfer of episcopal power to other members of the clergy. The existence of baptisteries of the so-called rural type of churches is an occurrence that was present in the entire area of the Balkans. The diffusion of these baptisteries was in accordance with the intention of Justinian I to finally finish the process of Christianisation of the non-urbanised parts of the Balkan Peninsula. With the invasion of barbarian tribes from the north, most prominently the Avars and the Slavs, at the end of the 6th and the beginning of the 7th century, this relatively long process of Christianisation of the pagan, already Romanised, autochthonous population was interrupted in its final phase, when the entire urban structure of the prefecture of Illyricum was destroyed, and with it the already widespread and firmly established church organisation.

3

Objects Used in Early Christian Liturgical Rites

In the period of early Christianity, objects dedicated to a cult were of particular significance, indicating not only a devotion to the church but also the economic potential of the ecclesiastic community. Numerous church treasures found in the various parts of the empire, among which are items used in liturgical rituals and countless gifts, including votive objects of great value and income from properties that were donated to the church, were the main source of the church's wealth in the first centuries of its establishment. The construction of lavish sacral structures with equally rich decoration was particularly characteristic of the eastern part of the empire. In the early period of Christianity, the Christogram was the most common symbol that indicated the Christian character of an object. Later, at the end of the 5th and in the 6th century, Christian symbolism was an integral part of silverware decoration used in liturgical rituals (chalices, bowls, spoons etc.). In the area of the Roman provinces of *Moesia Prima* and *Dacia Ripensis,* there has been found a large collection of various Early Christian liturgical items, along with objects with a wide variety of purposes whose form or decoration indicates a Christian attribution (Map 3.1).

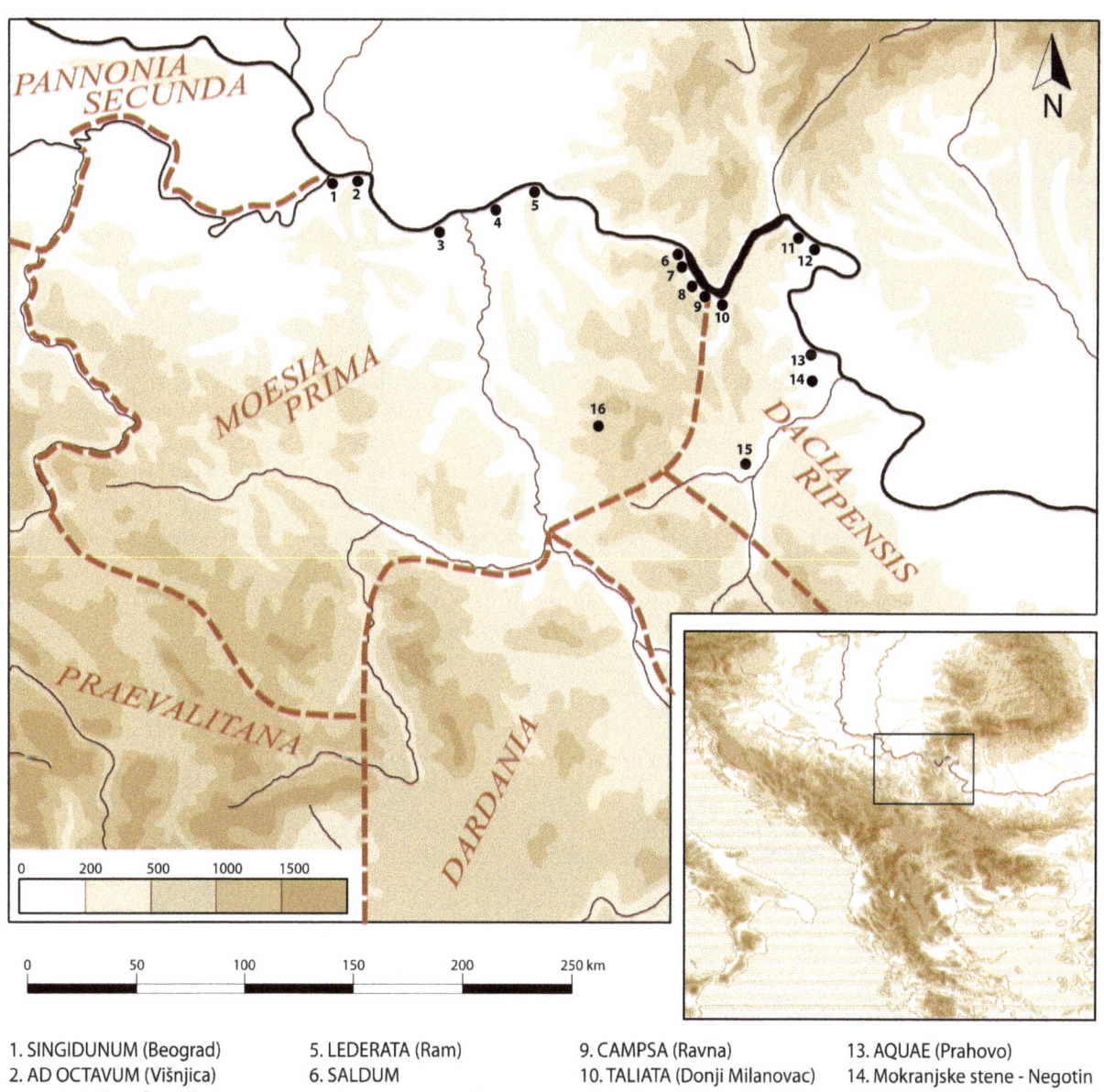

1. SINGIDUNUM (Beograd)
2. AD OCTAVUM (Višnjica)
3. VINCEIA (Smederevo)
4. VIMINACIUM (Stari Kostolac)
5. LEDERATA (Ram)
6. SALDUM
7. Manastir - Gospođin Vir
8. SMORNA (Boljetin)
9. CAMPSA (Ravna)
10. TALIATA (Donji Milanovac)
11. DIANA (Karataš)
12. PONTES (Kostol)
13. AQUAE (Prahovo)
14. Mokranjske stene - Negotin
15. ROMULIANA (Gamzigrad)
16. Panjevac - Despotovac

Map 3.1. The sites with Early Christian findings in the provinces of *Moesia Prima* and *Dacia Ripensis.*

3.1. Liturgical vessels

Vessels used in liturgical rites in the Early Christian church had the epithet of "holy", thus indicating their importance in ecclesiastic ceremonies. The most important liturgical rite is the act of the Eucharist, and it is performed with the use of consecrated bread and wine (the bread symbolising the body of Christ, and the wine the blood of Christ, in memory of Christ's sacrifice: Matthew 26, 26–28; Mark 14, 22–24). The ritual items placed on the altar for this ceremony were: chalices and pitchers for wine and water, colanders and bowls for the consecrated bread.

The quality of liturgical vessels owned by a church was a reflection, in a way, of the property status of the members of that church community. In northern Syria and the eastern part of Asia Minor, notable hoards were discovered with extremely valuable silver church vessels, which represented gifts from certain richer members of the ecclesiastic community. These numerous and precious hoards of church objects are indicative not only of devotion to religious institutions, but also of the accessibility of silver and the economic development of these areas in the Late Antique period. Aside from the items used in liturgical rites, the discovered church hoards also contained numerous gifts, among which were votive objects of great value obtained from donors or as revenue from properties bequeathed to the church. The contribution of the believers, members of the ecclesiastic community and pilgrims, aside from the revenue from church properties, was one of the main sources of the wealth of the church, and it was used for the building and decorating of sacral buildings. Many of these items can be precisely chronologically determined into the middle of the 6th century, due to the presence of control stamps or inscriptions with the names of the gift givers.

On a large number of silver vessels (chalices, bowls, pitchers, spoons) intended for liturgical rites, we can find the symbol of Christ's monogram, usually engraved. Unlike the late antique silver vessels from the early 4th century, later, during the 5th century, and especially during the early Byzantine period in the 6th century, Christian symbolism was an integral part of the decorative content, either in terms of the ornaments or the content of the inscriptions, which were relatively common in this period.

During the reign of Anastasius I (491–518 AD), who was the author of an important monetary reform, a system of strict rules was established for the use of stamps, which continued to function in the workshops of Constantinople during the time of his heir, Justinian I (527–565 AD), who established five official stamps for silver control (Cruiskshank Dodd 1961, 23–35). A firm state hierarchy was established, with a *comes sacrarum largitionum* at the head of it (Kent 1961, 35–45). Aside from the stamps, they also controlled coins. An important centre of silver trade in this period was Constantinople.

Silver vessels – chalices and bowls

During the Late Antique period, *Viminacium* was the capital of the province of *Moesia Prima* and the Episcopal See. Among other things, a rich collection of silver vessels discovered in the territory of this city also speaks of the wealth and importance of the city in the period from the 4th to the 6th century. We can distinguish a rich collection of silverware. Five silver chalices on a tall conical foot with a cover (two of them preserved) were made using the casting technique with engraving (Fig. 3.1). All five of these vessels have a recipient in the shape of a minor hemispherical bowl with a groove to accommodate a lid. The lids are completely flat, with a tall handle in the shape

Figure 3.1. Kostolac–*Viminacium*. Collection of silver chalices (5). (Documentation of the National Museum of Serbia).

of a hoop. In the recess of the lid of one of the vessels, a cursive inscription was engraved: *matrona*. On another chalice, there is the same cursive inscription in the recess of the foot (Popović 1994, 51, kat. 277–281).

In a famous hoard from Canoscio, in Italy, we find similar types of vessels that were most probably used during the rite of the Eucharist (Milojčić 1970, 122). Aside from these examples from Italy, one hemispherical bowl, on a tall foot, is reminiscent of these chalices; it was discovered in Carthage, and it is kept at the British Museum in London (Dalton 1901, 80, kat. 361). The profile of the foot of a silver chalice discovered at the site of Riha, near Aleppo, in Syria is very similar to the foot of the silver vessels with a lid from *Viminacium* (Ross 1962, no. 9, pl. X).[27] On the basis of the five identified stamps on the inner side of the foot, used to guarantee the quality of the silver, the chalice is attributed to one of the workshops in Constantinople during the reign of Justinian I. The control stamps from this chalice enabled a precise dating into the year 542 AD by means of a hexagonal monogram of Justinian and Peter, which most probably refers to the *comes sacrarum largitionum* from that period (Cruiskshank Dodd 1961, 69, cat. 8). Abundant hoards of silverware used in liturgical rites were found in the north of Syria and eastern parts of Asia Minor. They were probably gifts from wealthier members of the church community. One collection of artefacts from Hama contained chalices, strainers, ladles, spoons, fans and lamps. The official stamps on these items enable a very precise dating to the early Byzantine period (Mundell Mango 1986, 68–73, fig. 1, 2; Israeli, Mevorah, eds. 2000, 88).[28]

Small vessels in the shape of a hemispherical bowl, known as *Schüssel mit Kugelrandvezierung* are widespread in Late Antique period finds. They have been discovered in hoards ranging from Britain to the countries of the Eastern Mediterranean. An engraved Christogram of a bowl from *Viminacium* on two places on the lower side of the rim indicates the Christian use of this bowl (Fig. 3.2). Numerous analogies have been found: in finds from Traprain Law in Scotland (Hartley *et al.* eds. 2006, 236–237, cat. 240–243); from Kerch in Crimea (*Panticapaeum*) (*Spätantike und frühbyzantinische Silbergefässe* 1978, 134, Abb. 42); in the vicinity of Latakiya in Syria (Mundell Mango 1998, 214, fig. 12); from Palmira (Cruikshank Dodd 1961, cat. 81a). The control stamp on the vessel from Palmira, and on some other specimens, enables a dating of this type of vessel to the last quarter of the 4th century (Cruikshank Dodd 1961, cat. 82b). Based on these analogies, as well as the engraved Christogram, we could date the bowl from *Viminacium* to the same period.

Among liturgical vessels from *Viminacium*, two shallow bowls with a horizontally profiled rim stand out (Figs.

Figure 3.2. Kostolac–*Viminacium.* Silver bowl with Christ monogram. (Documentation of the National Museum of Serbia).

3.3 a-b). On the outer side of the base, on two opposite ends, a rectangular cross-shaped stamp is imprinted, with the letters *b* and *z* around it (Ilić, Jeremić 2018, 251–253; Kondić 1994, 318, 319). The letter *z* could be the start of the *zeses* acclamation, which is common on early Christian inscriptions (Kondić 1994, 66).[29] Considering the fact that the finding conditions are unknown for these vessels,[30] and since this finding also contains four spoons, these two bowls could belong to the same chronological timeframe, the 5th–6th century. A deep silver bowl, with a thick rim and engraved cross on it, with a monogram, also belongs to the repertoire of late antique bowls.[31] The second vessel from *Viminacium* is somewhat lower, but this need not be the actual state of things, since the actual dimensions cannot be determined with precision because of the severe damage on the rim of the edge of the foot. Considering the fact that the finding conditions are unknown for the two described vessels,[32] and since this finding also contains four spoons, which can be considered a set of sorts, consequently, these two bowls could also belong to the chronological timeframe, the 5th–6th century.

The repertoire of Late Antique bowls on a tall conical hollow foot is joined by a deep silver bowl, with a thick annular rim, from unknown site, kept in the National Museum in Belgrade (Fig. 3.4). There is an engraved cross on it, with monogram. The arms of the cross end with the

---

[27] Now the silver chalice from Riha is in the Dumbarton Oaks Collection in Washington.
[28] More about these vessels see: Ilić, Jeremić 2018, 249–250.
[29] The Latin *vivas* would correspond to the acclamation of *zeses*.
[30] The collection of Christian objects from *Viminacium* that consists of two bowls and four spoons represents an accidental find that was purchased by the National Museum of Serbia (two bowls and three spoons); the fourth spoon of the same type is a part of the collection of the National Museum in Požarevac.
[31] The bowl is from unknown site, kept in the National Museum in Belgrade. For more about these bowls see: (Ilić, Jeremić 2018, 251–253).
[32] The collection of Christian objects from *Viminacium* that consists of two bowls and four spoons represents an accidental find that came into the National Museum of Serbia as purchased (two bowls and three spoons); the fourth spoon of the same type is a part of the collection of the National Museum in Požarevac.

Late Antiquity and Early Christianity in the Roman Provinces of Moesia Prima and Dacia Ripensis

Figure 3.4. Unknown site. Silver bowl with monogram. (Documentation of the National Museum of Serbia).

Bronze pitcher

At the Roman fort of *Pontes,* near Kostol, on the Iron Gate section of the Danube Limes in the province of *Dacia Repensis*, a hoard of medieval iron tools was found in the layer between a house from the second half of the 9th century and a house from the 11th century (Popović 2015, 121–123). The most typical item from this hoard was a bronze pitcher with a biblical inscription (Fig. 3.5a-c). Engraved on the neck of the vessel there is an inscription – φονη κυρειου επει τον υδατον (The voice of the Lord is upon the waters), which is a part of the third verse of the 29th Psalm of King David (Popović 2015, 123, fig. 1). There are several assumptions about the dating and origin of this liturgical vessel. According to the most recent interpretation, the pitcher was dated to the end of the 6th and the beginning of the 7th century (Popović 2015, 127).[33]

3.2. Censers

As part of liturgical objects, censers had an important role in liturgical rites, starting from the Early Christian period. Their function remains the same even today. The custom of burning incense was recorded as early as in the pharaonic tradition. We encounter it later in pagan cults, but also in the Old Testament.[34] The religious burning of incense was considered a symbolical act of bowing down before God. Some scholars believe that, in the beginning, Christians rejected the burning of incense, considering it unworthy of the Christian liturgy because of its pagan connotations.[35] At a later point, however, the Christian church did accept this custom. Up until the 4th century we have no reliable reports on the use of incense during liturgical rites, and

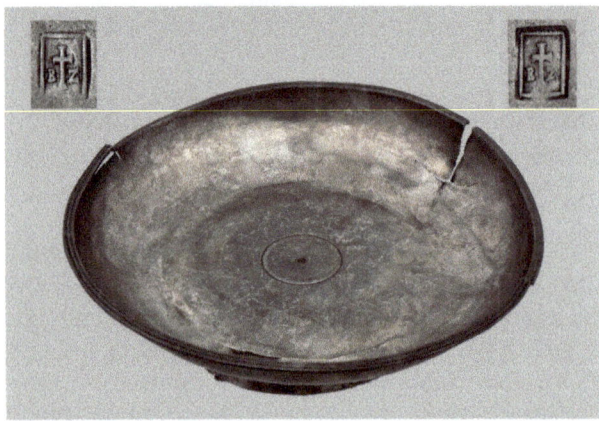

Figure 3.3. a-b Kostolac–*Viminacium*. Silver bowls with two stamps in the form of Latin cross (2). (Documentation of the National Museum of Serbia).

letters *z* (down), *o* (left), *c* (up) and *a* (right) (Kondić 1994, 66). Such crosses with monograms were typical for the Byzantium in the 6th century, and they most commonly contained proper names. The monogram can be read as + Ζωσα. It is a proper name that can be interpreted as either a female name in the nominative case – Ζωσα, or as a male name in the possessive genitive case. Both these names were common in late antique onomastics (Diehl 1961, 4029). Cross-shaped monograms appeared from the times of Justinian I, hence, that could also have been the time when these vessels were made (Cruiskshank Dodd 1961, 23–35).

Silver vessels from *Viminacium* are characterised by the simplicity of the shape and the reduced ornamentation, most often consisting of several concentric circles. Vessels are mostly made of lower quality silver, and are similar in their form and dimensions. In comparison with objects originating from the East, our specimens look very modest, both in their production technique and their decorative themes. On the basis of analogies, we can conclude that these vessels in the form of a chalice, by their style, show particular features that could be said to be a combination of existing forms of eastern origin with a local tradition, which leads to the conclusion that the vessels might have been manufactured in the local workshops of *Viminacium*.

---

[33] For more about the appearance and chronological determination of the bronze pitcher see: Ilić, Jeremić 2018, 255–258.

[34] Incense originates from India, and the Jewish people called it λίβανον, *libanum*. Aside from this, there was also the name of υμίαμα, from the word ύω, which means to sacrifice, because it was used during the offering of sacrifices.

[35] It was used during pagan offerings of sacrifices, but also in Jewish rites, when one of the priests would burn incense during the sacrifice at the golden altar.

Objects Used in Early Christian Liturgical Rites

the act of incense burning can be reliably linked to the Christian liturgy only from the 4th century (Mirković 1965, 319). The oldest mention of censers as items used in Christian rites comes from Constantine's period. Thus, *Liber Pontificalis* mentions censers gifted by Constantine to the Lateran church (Cabrol et Leclercq 1922, 23). At a later point, during the period of Justinian I, their presence was witnessed on monumental mosaics from Ravenna, in the churches of St. Apollinaire in Classe and St. Vitale. In the Christian cult, the burning of incense, which fills the area of the church with its fragrance, plays an important role. According to the Church Fathers, it is a general symbol of prayer, worshiping and offering sacrifice to God. The burning of incense was prescribed as an act of preparation and consecration, or as an expression of sacred reverence. During liturgical rites, but also in household use, different types of censers were used for that purpose. They were mostly made of metal (bronze), but also from stone or baked earth. Censers usually consist of a round recipient, although they can also be square, hexagonal or conical, with three rings through which three chains pass, attached at the top. Most of the shapes also have a round foot. A large number of bronze censers have a decoration consisting of images illustrating events from the life of Christ. Those scenes are often made in a simplified manner, hence, it is sometimes difficult to decipher them, with details sometimes additionally applied after the casting.

The censer from *Romuliana* represents a part of a hoard in which, aside from the censer, a polycandeleon, a candelabrum, and a mushroom-shaped fittings were also found (Fig. 3.6c). This hoard was discovered in one of the towers of the older fortification. The hoard was most probably put aside in the final quarter of the 6th century, in times of frequent barbaric intrusions into the territory of the Empire (Janković 1983, 135). The censer is made of bronze, hexagonal in shape, with a simple decoration in the form of a profiled base and a rim. It was set on three feet ending in the shape of lion paws. It was suspended on three chains, which were attached at the top with a link in a figure-of-eight shape. There was a rectangular opening on one of the sides of the censer that was closed at a later point.

From the Episcopal residence in Stobi in Northern Macedonia, we have an example analogous to the one from *Romuliana*, which has a decoration in the form of an engraved cross on the sides. It was dated into the end of the 5th century (Mano-Zisi 1962, 103, sl. 3). The Coptic Museum in Cairo keeps a bronze censer that is identical in form to our finding. It was suspended on three chains, attached at the top with a ring. The three feet also end in the form of lion paws (Stryzgowski 1904, No. 9116, Taf. XXXII). Another censer similar to the finding from *Romuliana* comes from an unknown site, and it is now kept at the Bayerischen Sammlungen in Munich (Baumstark, ed. 1998, 49, Kat. 39). From these examples, we can see that there was a considerable uniformity in the production of these censers, which undoubtedly indicates

Figure 3.5. a-c Kostol–*Pontes*. Bronze pitcher, view and details. (Documentation of the National Museum of Serbia).

the existence of production centres, from where they were distributed across the Empire.

The Belgrade City Museum keeps a bronze censer with a hemispherical recipient, with three circular openings for hanging. The censer belongs to the Dunjic Collection, and it probably originates from the region of the mountain of Kosmaj, to the south of Belgrade (Janković 1997, 325).

We can assume that this censer also arrived in the territory of the province of *Moesia Prima* as an import. The censer represents one of the rare Christian findings from the area of antique *Singidunum*.

An exceptional example of a censer comes from the demolished medieval church in the vicinity of Kursumlija, in southern Serbia, which is kept at the National Museum

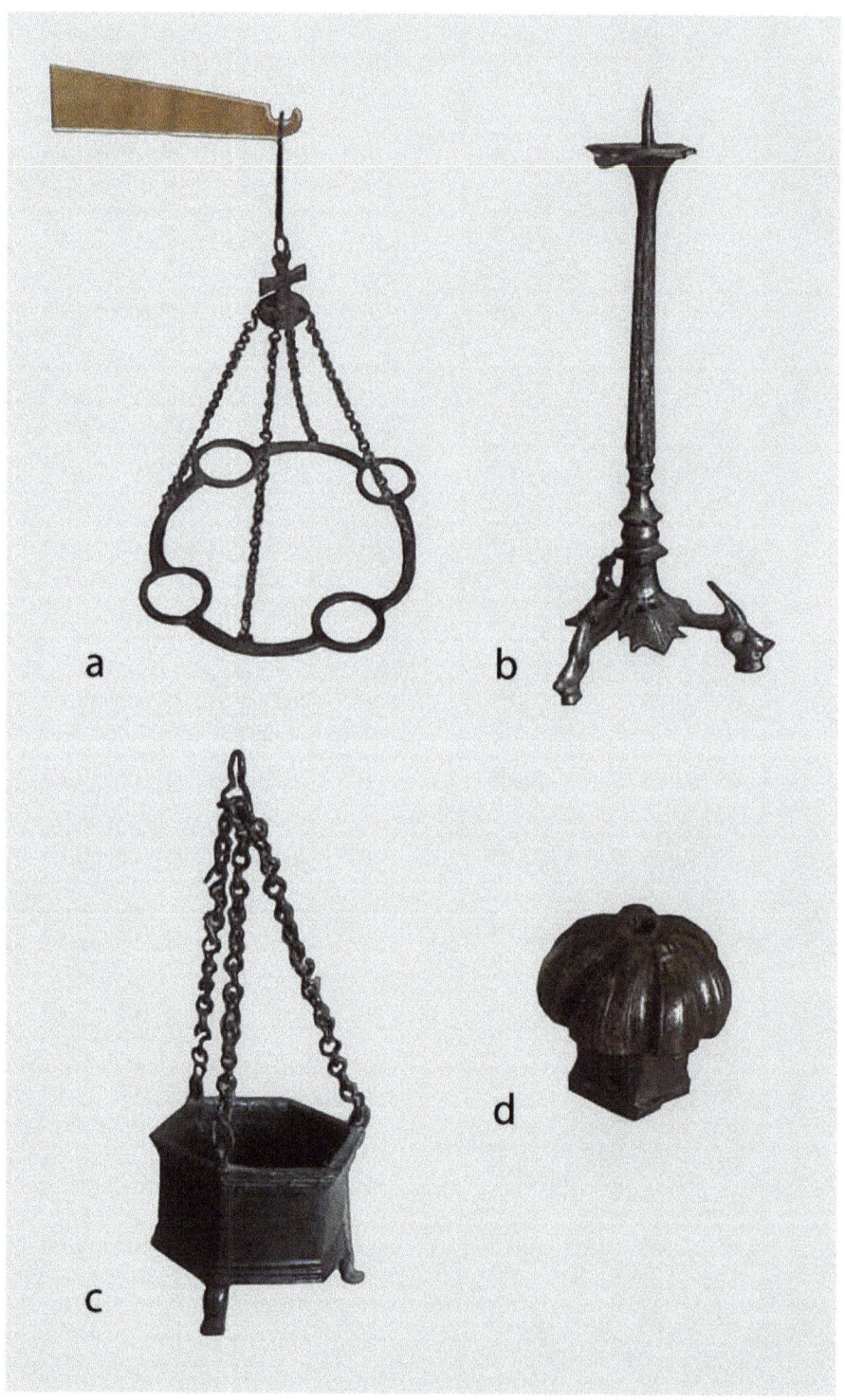

Figure 3.6. a-d Gamzigrad–*Romuliana*. A hoard of church items: a – polycandelon; b – candelabrum; c – censer; d – mushroom-shaped fittings. (Documentation of the National Museum in Zaječar).

in Belgrade today.³⁶ The bronze censer has a spherical shape, on a round foot, without a preserved lid. The chains were fastened onto three links, and they were probably attached under a small lid at the top, as can be seen on preserved examples. The censer is divided into three ornamental belts (Figs. 3.7a-b). An undecorated band runs along the rim, separated by an accentuated decorative rib. The central belt contains a relief with cast representations of religious content. The third ornamental belt is located under this part; it is circular in shape, with a relief in the shape of a flower with petals (corolla), with a hollow foot at the centre, and another seven-petal flower at the bottom. The relief representations with images from the life of Christ cover the entire central portion of the censer and they contain six episodes from the New Testament: the Annunciation, the Visitation, the Nativity, the Annunciation to the Shepherds, the Baptism and the Crucifixion.

Censers with similar shapes and dimensions, and with similar images from the life of Christ, have been found on a great number of sites, both in the Mediterranean area (Egypt, Syria, eastern Turkey), and also deeper in the inner parts of the Eurasian territory (southern Russia, Caucasus, and Central Asia), (Gonosová and Kondoleon 1994, 276, note 6).³⁷ In the area of Northern Illyricum, a censer from the vicinity of Kursumlija represents a unique finding.

In Syria, in the vicinity of Damascus, a censer was discovered similar to our example, both in terms of the form and the content of the relief representations (Dalton 1901, 107–108, cat. 540). There are also scenes of the Annunciation, the Baptism, the Crucifixion, and the Holy Virgin Mary at the Holy Sepulchre. A censer that should be mentioned in particular is an example from Egypt, which is kept at the Virginia Museum of Fine Arts in Richmond, with compositions illustrating events from the life of Christ (Gonosová and Kondoleon 1994, cat. 95). The censer was preserved in its entirety, including all three chains. On the basis of analogous examples, as well as the iconographic analysis of the decorative elements present on this censer, it is most probable that it originates from Egypt, as a product of Coptic workshops from the late 7ᵗʰ or the beginning of the 8ᵗʰ century (Gonosová and Kondoleon 1994, 277). From the Louvre, we have a large number of censers of various types, among which there are examples with relief representations depicting events from the life of Christ (Bénazeth 1992, No 11270, 11709, 11710). They all originate from Egypt, and they are chronologically determined into the so-called Islamic period, in the 7ᵗʰ–8ᵗʰ century.³⁸ It is very characteristic for many censers from the period after the 7ᵗʰ century that their decorative motifs and a figural expression were, at that point, very simplified, although they were still partially under influences from the 6ᵗʰ and the 7ᵗʰ century, hence, they were gradually losing their clear traits in many details.

As was already mentioned, a large number of censers of this type have been found to date. A considerable number of them originates from Egypt and Syria, but also from eastern Turkey, southern Russian and from the Caucasus, as well as Central Asia (Gonosová and Kondoleon 1994, 276). Even though they are not completely identical in their form, their relief decorations with images from the cycle of the life of Christ were executed in a style that was so similar that it indicates their common origin. Scenes depicted on censers vary in number (from four to nine), with representations from the life of Christ standing out.

Since representations from these censers are more or less identical to those from pilgrim ampullae, in which ointments were carried from the churches of Jerusalem or consecrated earth from places linked to the passion of Christ, on the basis of iconographic analyses of relief representations, the more or less accepted theory today is that the origin of this type of censers, and ampullae, should be sought in the Syrian-Palestinian artistic milieu, i.e. in the context of art intended for the pilgrims in the Holy Land (Ljubinković-Ćorović 1950, 82–83). Hence, we may conclude that censers represented items made especially for the pilgrims in the Holy Land, same as the ampullae were made. They have, first and foremost, compositions that illustrate events from the life of Christ, which unfolded in places where a church was erected in memory of those given events.

When we speak of this type of censer, there are still no precise answers to the question of their chronological determination. Ampullae are a rather homogenous group of items, which can be dated with a lot of certainty into the period from the second half of the 6ᵗʰ century up to the first half of the 8ᵗʰ century, even though they are akin, censers can have a particular distinction between themselves, indicating production that lasted over a longer period of time, starting from the 6ᵗʰ century and all the way until the early Middle Ages. Similarly, unlike ampullae, which often contain inscriptions that can enable rather certain dating, this type of inscription is quite rare in censers, which renders their chronological determination rather difficult. An important trait of censers made after the 7ᵗʰ century is their decoration, which is characterised by simplified figural representations, which, even though they were still under the influence of the Byzantine art of the 6ᵗʰ and the 7ᵗʰ century, gradually lost certain characteristic traits, moving towards a schematisation of those representations. A characteristic of this type of censer is a uniformity of style, in spite of different production dates, as well as the fact that a large number of them was preserved. We can also note that the artistic style on these censers did not change abruptly, especially on censers discovered in the Mediterranean region, after

---

³⁶ The censer is kept at the Medieval Collection of the National Museum of Serbia. Since we do not know the original place of use of this censer, although it was found in the province of *Dacia Mediterranea*, we believe that it should be discussed more, being a very interesting finding, deserving of our intention.

³⁷ To date, around a hundred censers of this type have been discovered.

³⁸ "The Islamic period" in the context that we speak of was characterised by changes in the artistic expression of the Coptic production, which began immediately after the conquest of Egypt by the Arabs.

Figure 3.7. a-b Kuršumlija, Pepeljevac. Bronze censer with relief depictions from the life of Christ. (Documentation of the National Museum of Serbia).

great political and religious changes that occurred with the arrival of the Arabs in this territory in the middle of the 7th century.

The study of art intended for the pilgrims in the Holy Land shows that items made for this purpose did not have the function of being merely a "memento" of their sojourn in the Holy Land, instead, they had an apotropaic meaning too (Israeli and Mevorah, eds. 2000, 201). On this topic, we may assume that the original censers were replaced in time, where it was necessary, with replicas, which would explain the large number of preserved censers. As these censers were made in a territory that was under Arab rule, where contact with the Byzantine art could not have been maintained as had previously been the case, the new stylistic and artistic movements of the Byzantine art would not reach these regions, hence, the decoration of later examples would only maintain the original content of the compositions and traces of the style from the 6th and the 7th century.

Certain authors who have dealt with this topic are prone to assume that they continued to be produced after the 7th century as well, since the preserved examples indicate that those were most probably Syrian–Palestinian copies, produced in different regions of the former Byzantine Empire (Gonosová and Kondoleon 1994, 277). It is characteristic for these censers that, with their decorative content and their already simplified figural expression, they would gradually lose clear traits of the style of the early Byzantine censers from the 6th–7th century, although they still kept the original compositional scheme.

Bearing all of this in mind, we can note that the relief representations on the censer from Kuršumlija, are quite close to the Byzantine art from the 6th–7th century.

However, we can hardly say that it is an example that was made in the Holy Land, or in any of the Syrian-Palestinian workshops. We could sooner say, on the basis of stylistic traits of the relief representations, as well as their similarity with several examples of Egyptian provenance, that it was a Coptic product, made in one of the Egyptian production centres. The previously mentioned opinion of certain authors, according to which the censer was a Syrian–Palestinian product from the 6th–7th century, would thus be revised (Ljubinković-Ćorović 1950, 83). On the basis of all that was mentioned here, it would seem that the censer is indeed somewhat more recent and that it could be dated into the so-called Islamic period, that is to say, into the late 7th century or the beginning of the 8th century.

The question of the presence of this censer in the area of Northern Illyricum in the mentioned period remains open. Was it an item that represented a part of a hidden hoard or perhaps confirmation of the existence of a church organisation in this region in the end of the 7th and the beginning of the 8th century? According to preserved written sources (*Notitia* I, Ms. Hierosol. Patr. 39), from the times of the reign of Heraclius, the provinces that were a part of the Empire in the 5th and the 6th century are not mentioned in *Notitia* I (Živković 2004, 58, note 201). Firstly, the provinces that were a part of the archbishopric of *Iustiniana Prima* are missing. For the time being, it remains unknown just what really happened to the episcopacies from this territory and whether some of them continued to perform their function. The fact remains that during the 7th and the 8th century Byzantium could not have influenced events in the inner parts of the Balkan Peninsula in any significant manner, because it was occupied with the war with the Arabs in the East in this period, and starting from the year 680 AD, the Bulgarians appeared as a new enemy to the west from Thrace.

3.3. Spoons

Very little was written in our scholarly literature about spoons as items that were probably used during liturgical rites, therefore, it is necessary to provide some general information on the topic (Tatić-Đurić 1967, 243–245; Kondić 1994, 65–67). Silver spoons from the period from the second half of the 5th to the 7th century are sorted into three types, with their names being determined on the basis of their eponymous sitesm (Bierbrauer 1975, 180–188):

- the Desana type, named after the hoard discovered in Desana, in Italy;
- the Sutton Hoo type, named after the eponymous site in the county of Kent, in England;
- the Krefeld-Gellep type, named following the finding of a silver spoon in a male prince grave in the valley of the Rhine, in Germany.

All three listed types of spoons are similar in form, and they are also chronologically contemporary. The presence of different symbols or inscriptions are the characteristics of all three types of these spoons. Engraved motifs, most commonly the cross, appear often on the disc of the Desana type spoons. Christograms and monograms, as well as other inscriptions, are also present. On the upper side of the beginning of the handle, proper names can be engraved, more commonly Latin ones, although they can be written in the Greek alphabet as well. Proper names can also appear on recipients, and different Christian symbols. This type of spoon was widespread across the larger portion of the European continent, from Russia, across the Danube Valley and the Rhine Valley all the way to England, and in the south, all the way to the Mediterranean.[39] The finding conditions are very heterogeneous. Silver spoons can come from settlements, graves – both male and female, and they can also be parts of hoards. Based on the level of research achieved so far, it was noted that grave goods containing silver spoons are more present to the north of the Alps, while to the south of the Alps, in the Mediterranean region, silver spoons are mostly present in hoards and settlements, most commonly urban agglomerations or fortifications.

Four silver spoons that are part of the previously mentioned collection of silver liturgical items originate from *Viminacium* (Fig. 3.8).[40] The spoons have an ovoid shape, and on the transition point that connects the handle to the recipient, a monogram is engraved, which, according to some authors, can be read as *Enneus* (Tatić-Đurić 197, 244). This ligature with a monogram is similar to those on stamps in the period from 491 to 602 AD (Cruikshank Dodd 1961, 104, pl. 250). Another silver spoon with a Christian symbol originates from *Romuliana*, in the province of *Dacia Ripensis*. The recipient of this spoon is decorated with a Christogram made using the punching technique (Živić 2003, 71, fig. 31).

The similarity of vessels and spoons from *Viminacium* and *Romuliana* with findings from the famous church treasure of Canoscio in Italy (Milojčić 1970, 122, Abb. 9/1, 11), in which items with emphasised Christian symbols (Christogram, fish, lamb) have also been found, indicates that these objects could also be parts of church liturgical vessels. According to their characteristics, they could be typologically determined into the Desana type, characterised by a disc in the transition piece that connects the recipient of spoon to the handle (Bierbrauer 1975, 204–207, Tab. V–XVII). Usually, various Christian symbols or inscriptions were engraved on the disc, as is also the case in the specimens from *Viminacium* (Ilić, Jeremić 2018, 253–255).

From the territory that encompasses today's Romania, as well as the provinces that spread to the south of the Danube, we can also encounter spoons similar to the findings from *Viminacium*. Thus, three silver examples

---

[39] In the comprehensive study on silver spoons, the author presented numerous examples gathered from the area of the entire Europe (396 spoons were presented in his paper), with all possible combinations of decorative content and inscriptions, *cf.* Milojčić 1970, 111–133.
[40] Three of them are housed in the National Museum in Belgrade, and the fourth is in the National Museum in Požarevac.

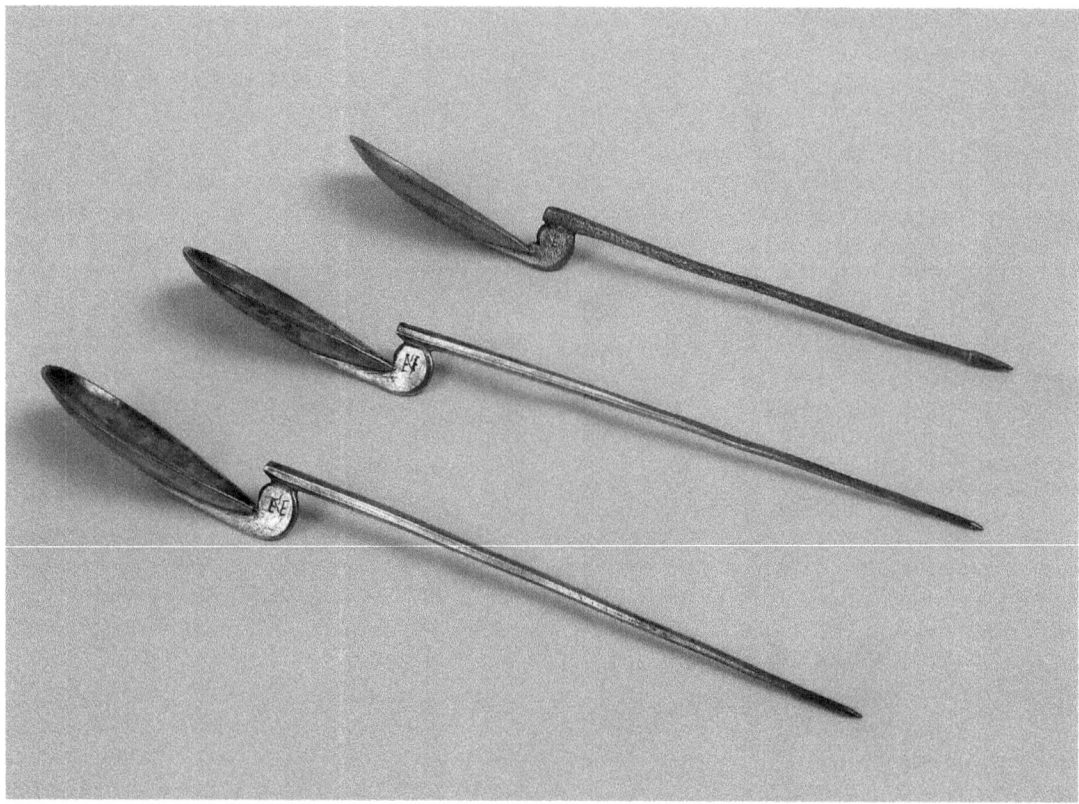

Figure 3.8. Kostolac–*Viminacium*. Silver spoons. (Documentation of the National Museum of Serbia).

were discovered at the site of Botoşani, in Romania, along with a silver censer (Teodor 2001, 118, Fig. 3/7–9). Also from Romania, there are examples discovered in Orşova (*Dierna*) (Rădulescu et Lungu 1989, 2596), while an extraordinary finding, containing six silver examples, comes from a hoard discovered in the antique fortification of *Suçidava*, near Celei (Rădulescu et Lungu 1989, 2594, 2595, 2597, figs. 23–25). The inscriptions from these spoons indicate their Christian attribution, although the question as to whether they were used in the Christian cult, in the rites of the Eucharist, or they were in profane use, as part of the cutlery, remains open. Chronologically speaking, they are somewhat older than the examples from our catalogue and they are dated into the second half of the 4th century. Almost identical examples to our spoons come from Porto, Cioara, and Augsburg Milojčić 1970, Abb. 7/3, 5, 6, 7), having in common the presence of a monogram on the transition point from the recipient to the handle. They are dated into the 6th and the beginning of the 7th century. An accidental finding of a silver spoon from *Siscia* should also be mentioned, which, unlike our examples, has a cross engraved on the disk. As this spoon is analogous to the findings from Desana, it is dated into the first half of the 6th century (Simoni 1988, 81. T. 1, 2).

The Dumbarton Oaks Collection contains seven extremely luxuriously made silver spoons with a monogram on the disk that connects the recipient with the handle. The inscriptions on the handle, made using the niello technique, indicate the Christian character of these spoons, most probably used during the rites of the Eucharist, considering the content of the text (Ross 1962, cat. 13, Pl. XVII). In fact, the names from the inscriptions clearly indicate that they are names of the Apostles (Thomas, Luke, Mark, Peter, Matthew, Philip and Paul) and it is most probable that the original number of these spoons was twelve. They most probably originated from Antioch, and they are dated into the late 6th and the beginning of the 7th century (Mundell Mango 1986, cat. 49–56). Long-handled silver spoon hase been found in the treasure from Traprain Law in Scotland, naw housed in the National Museums of Scotlans in Edinburgh (E. Hartley *et al*. eds. 2006, 239–240, cat. 248).

As we mentioned at the beginning, the function of spoons has not been entirely defined in scholarly literature. While certain authors define and observe them as items belonging to the Christian cult, used in liturgical rites during the act of the Eucharist (Milojčić 1970, 112–113), others attribute a profane function to them, as being pieces of cutlery (Foltiny 1974, 266), which may seem a perfectly reasonable explanation at first, since precious silver spoons with rich decorations have been in profane use on the tables of the rich in various epochs. Thus, some of the authors strongly negate any cult application, since silver spoons were mostly limited to richer female graves in the area to the north of the Alps, among the Germanic people, which speaks, in a way, against the use of these items in purposes linked to the Eucharist (Milojčić 1970, 111, note 1, 2). Certain authors negate the cult purpose of spoons with Christian symbols or inscriptions because other items for everyday use can also appear bearing Christian symbols, without that necessarily being an indicator of their use in liturgical rites and, on the other hand, their appearance in graves along with vessels used for food and drink would indicate a non-Christian attribution (Simoni 1988, 81–82). Also, there is still a dilemma as to whether a certain number of spoons that were a part of grave inventories represented profane offerings during family commemorations, as an expression of social acknowledgement, or an apotropaic character was attributed to them, with the spoon serving as an amulet against evil to its owner (Milojčić 1970, 126–127). In this context, we should also mention an interesting observation by K. Simoni, who compares the appearance of silver spoons to helmets of the Baldenheim type (Simoni 1988, 82). She believes that a similarity exists in the appearance of various Christian symbols on these items, which could be a reflection of the spirit of the time in which they were created. On the other hand, bearing in mind inscriptions and different Christian representations present on many examples (Milojčić 1970, Abb. 7, 8, 9), it would be difficult to accept the previous interpretations that spoons had no application whatsoever in the cult sphere of Christianity. Christian symbols on them evidently speak of their application in liturgical practices. The fact that one part of the spoons with inscriptions was not a mere gift with apotropaic symbols or proverbs handed out during profane family celebrations is also indicated by a group of spoons with the names of the Apostles, which were discovered individually (the previously mentioned group of seven examples from the Dumbarton Oaks Collection, which probably represent a part of a set of 12 spoons, which would correspond to the number of the Apostles). What should be pointed out here is the fact that spoons, most commonly silver ones, are used even today in Orthodox churches, during liturgical rites, namely, the rite of the Eucharist. Finally, we can ascertain that spoons intended for the Christian cult, as a rule, had a decoration on the inner side of the recipient or on the transition point from the recipient into the handle, most commonly a Christogram, which indicates a Christian attribution, or a text with a suitable liturgical content. Sometimes, we also have engraved representations with Christian symbols: fish, lamb, cross etc. All the stated facts clearly indicate that the spoons from *Viminacium* were used during the rites of the Eucharist and that their liturgical purpose is evident, as can be seen, first and foremost, from the engraved inscriptions and symbols.

3.4. Processional crosses

The cross is the main and most widespread Christian symbol that basically means the salvation of humankind through Christ's sacrifice. The entire liturgy is filled with this symbol. The Evangelists do not provide us with details about the cross on which Jesus was crucified, but they indicate its presence by mentioning the inscription placed above Christ's head: "Jesus of Nazareth, King of the Jews", (Matthew 27, 37; Luke 23, 38). The motif of the cross itself is a symbol recognisable for thousands of years before Christ and not only in the area where Christianity originated from, but in the wider Mediterranean region as well (Truhelka 1931, 24).[41] In Egypt, we encounter the symbolic meaning of the cross for the first time under the name of *anch*, which is in the shape of the letter "T", with a loop in the upper part. This symbol, called *crux ansata*, actually represents a hieroglyph with the meaning "life". Coptic art took on this symbol as an ideogram for Jesus Christ (Du Bourguet 1970, 158). After the crucifixion of Christ, the cross became the main symbol of the Christians and their faith in Christian salvation. It is the symbol of the passion of Christ and his victory over death, but also a symbol of the Christian faith. For Christians, it is a symbol of eternal life and, therefore, an object of constant worship.

The oldest representations of the cross as a symbol in Christian art appeared as painted decorations in the oldest catacombs, placed within the epitaphs to mark that the deceased were members of the Christian faith (Cabrol et Leclercq 1914, 3360–3369). Beginning with Constantine, when religious peace and tolerance were established and when Christianity became an acknowledged religion in the Empire, it started to be encircled by a wreath, most commonly one of laurel leaves. The victorious cross had an apotropaic meaning, as a weapon of sorts pointed against the enemy, carried by the *signophoros* (Baumstark, ed. 1998, 63). Starting from the 5th century, under the influence of the councils of Ephesus 431 AD and Chalcedon 451 AD (Kartašov 1995, 295–417), the cross became part of the dogma and official religion, retaining this attribute until today. In time, the cross became a part of the imperial privilege, thus, it was a common symbol on coins issued by Byzantine emperors, and it also appeared on the *exagia* of the state as an official mark of security and reliability. The motif of the cross is noticeable on numerous monuments of various purposes: carved or painted on the stone relief of public and private buildings, as a decorative motif on mosaics, painted on the walls of early Christian tombs, on objects made of wood and ivory, on objects of a religious character dedicated to liturgical activities or on objects that make up part of church inventory, on oil lamps, or stamped on objects that were in profane use. It is especially widespread on jewellery, primarily on Byzantine products of precious metals in the 5th and 6th century.

Based on the form of the crosses, it is possible to determine their use, or their function. Crosses of larger formats used during liturgical services, where they were carried in the church itself and around it, can be designated as processional, according to this function. Processional crosses can be made of gold, silver, bronze, lead or iron. Because of their great material value, gold ones were rarely preserved, while the silver ones were preserved in certain numbers, even those with gilding. In the early Byzantine period, decorations on the corners of the arms appeared, which could be in the shape of droplets, beads or discs.

---

[41] In prehistoric cultures, the cross represented one of the most typical motifs for inlaid ceramics; the ornamental motif of the cross was often widespread in the Mycenaean period, and we encounter this symbol across the entire Illyrian area in Hallstatt.

Figure 3.9. Gamzigrad–*Romuliana*. Processional cross. (Documentation of the National Museum in Zaječar).

Some examples of processional crosses were decorated with pendants, which would hang from the horizontal arm, in the form of small crosses, coloured beads, or the apocalyptic letters *α* and *ω* (Mottier et Bosson 1989–1990, 76–77, 93). Built-in implements near the bottom of the vertical arm, as well as decorative content that was often made using the niello technique, indicate that a given example is a processional cross. Even though this type of cross has no liturgical meaning like chalices or patens, used during the rites of the Eucharist, they still represented a precious part of the inventory of a church. They were kept at sanctuaries or, if made of precious metals, in separate church storage rooms.

From the territory of the province of *Dacia Ripensis*, a bronze cross came from *Romuliana*, which can be placed into the group of processional crosses (Fig. 3.9), (Janković 1983, 135, kat. 182; Živić 2003, kat. 387). The cross was discovered in a layer under a building with a corridor. The circular extensions at the corners of the arms, typical of the early Byzantine period, date this finding into the 6th century.

Examples of processional crosses come from the entire Mediterranean area. Thus, an exceptional example of a processional cross originates from the famous hoard from Phela, in Syria, which was made of silver, with an inscription in Greek.[42] The characteristic droplet-shaped extensions at the corners are similar to those from the finding from *Romuliana*. The example was dated into the end of the 6th and the beginning of the 7th century (Ross 1962, 19–20, Pl. XVIII/14).[43] An extremely luxurious silver processional cross comes from Luxor (Strzygowski 1904, No 7201, Taf. XXXIX).[44] With its elegant form, with a longer vertical arm, this cross also has droplet-shaped extensions at the ends of the arms, while an inscription in Greek runs along the horizontal and vertical arm. The implement from the lower arms was preserved in its entirety. Two examples from Hama, in Syria, are also of a similar form. They were dated into the 6th and the beginning of the 7th century (Mundell Mango 1986, 87, 90, fig. 7/2, 3; 8/1, 2).

As previously mentioned, procession crosses sometimes had pendants. Two such specimens of a processional cross made of lead come from *Viminacium*. Both crosses were hung on the lower edge of the horizontal arm, as indicated by holes on the upper vertical arm. According to some authors, such and similar crosses were donated to a church by believers as a pledge of their prayers with which they addressed it, or as a sign of gratitude (Marjanović-Vujović 1977, 11).

---

[42] The settlement of Phela has not been identified, but the hoard from Phela was named on the basis of an inscription on the cross and several other findings, originating from Syria.

[43] The cross is a part of the Dumbarton Oaks Collection.
[44] The cross is kept at the Coptic Museum in Cairo.

4

Objects Related to Christian Cult

4.1. Reliquaries

Collection and worship reliquaries already had an important role in the Christian cult during the first centuries of Christianity.[45] We can say that the appearance of reliquaries was directly connected to the creation and development of the Christian cult, which was based on the belief that the relics of saints and martyrs transferred their holiness onto all the things they would come in contact with. In order to bring the celestial altar closer to believers, it was at the end of the 4th century that the Church began to store parts of the physical remains of saints and martyrs in reliquaries, which were placed in special grave chambers (ενκαίνια).

The oldest example of the worship of relics was encountered with Saint Ignatius, the bishop of Antioch and a disciple of the Apostles, who died a martyr's death in Rome, at the beginning of the 2nd century. After his death, his relics were transferred to Antioch and kept in a casket. How common this observance of the relics of martyrs became in the 3rd century, we can learn from Eusebius, from his history of the Church, where he states how Christian martyrs were cast into the sea during the time of Diocletian's persecutions, in order to prevent the possibility of showing them respect (Mirković 1965, 187–188). After the 313 AD, when religious peace and tolerance were established, and when Christianity became an acknowledged religion, churches and chapels began to be built above the graves of martyrs, and they were then dedicated to them. According to the 7th Canon of the Seventh Ecumenical Council, held in Nicaea in 754 AD, relics of holy martyrs were to be placed or built into the altar (Αγία Τράπεζα) during the consecration of the church (Mirković 1965, 189). Thus, relics of saints acknowledged by the church authorities are presented for public reverence even today.

Relics themselves used to be kept in special boxes called reliquaries (*reliquarium*) and they were considered to be amulets that could provide protection and transfer blessings to believers. Early Christian reliquaries can be of different sizes and shapes, and also made from various materials: from precious metals, gold or silver, or bronze, lead, marble or stone, or baked clay. There were also cases when they had several compartments for different relics that were kept in them, as was the case with the reliquary from the church of Saint Stephen in Jerusalem (Cabrol et Leclercq 1948, 2323–2324, fig. 10606). Similarly, finds of certain reliquaries show that sometimes relics would be placed into smaller boxes, made of a precious metal, which were in turn placed inside larger boxes. As reliquaries had the symbolism of a grave, they were most commonly in the shape of a sarcophagus. The lids were also reminiscent of those from Roman sarcophagi, with gables and acroteria on the corners. They were often decorated with Christian symbols, most often crosses.

In most churches, reliquaries were found under the main altar, in a recess in the floor. Over time, they began to be set in a special place in churches that was determined for the cult of the holy relics – usually in a chamber near the apse. Similarly, relics were kept in niches in the walls, or under the altar, in crypts especially determined for the storage of holy objects, which enabled easier access to the relics. Their appearance is linked to the period from the 4th to the 6th century (Israeli and Mevorah eds. 2000, 77).

In the area of the Danube provinces, only one example of a silver reliquary has been discovered so far, originating from *Romuliana* (Fig. 4.1). The reliquary is of a simple, rectangular shape, made of silver sheet (Živić 2003, 71, sl. 32; Petković 2010, 199, sl. 173). The decoration consists of slanting lines, forming rhombi. On the front and the back, there is an engraved Latin cross in a protruding rhombus, with arms extended at the ends. Fields with engraved, slanting, parallel lines can be seen on the lateral sides. The lid is missing. The reliquary was an accidental find from the area in front of the northern gate of the fortification. The representation of a cross with arms extended at the ends of the reliquary indicates that it could have been made in the 6th century.

According to information gathered so far, most reliquaries in the shape of Roman sarcophagi should be attributed to the eastern Mediterranean production milieu. They were most commonly discovered in the area of south-eastern Europe and Asia Minor and they are dated mostly into the period from the 4th to the 6th century (Buschhausen 1971, 286–315). The region of today's Bulgaria should be especially singled out, because a total of 35 reliquaries has been discovered in this territory so far, with different forms, materials and made using different production techniques, thus, this represents a unique area not only in Europe, but in the entire Mediterranean region as well.[46] A considerable number of reliquaries have been discovered in churches, under the altar space, which indicates the important role they played in the cult itself. The marble reliquary discovered in the crypt under the altar of the church in the

---

[45] Holy relics and reliquaries (λείψανα, *reliquiae*) comprehend physical remains of the body of saints, as well as items that saints used in their lifetime or that were connected to them in some way.

[46] In contrast, it should be said that in the area of Asia Minor, only around twenty examples have been discovered, including the findings from Constantinople.

Figure 4.1. Gamzigrad–*Romuliana*. Silver reliquary. (Documentation of the National Museum in Zaječar).

vicinity of Varna, in Bulgaria (Minchev 2003, 15, no 1). Three silver reliquaries discovered within the area of the apse in the church of St. Sophia, in *Serdica* (today Sofia in Bulgaria) (Minchev 2003, 32–34, no. 22–24).

4.2. Gilded glass base

A gilded glass base with a portrait of a man, woman and a child, made in the *fondi d'oro* technique, originates from *Aquae* (today's Prahovo in eastern Serbia), in the province of *Dacia Ripensis*.[47] They are shown *en face*, with the Latin inscription *vivas in Deo* above them (Ružić 1994, kat.1194, T. XLIV/1) (Fig. 4.2).

The method of decorating in the *fondi d'oro* technique was common in the period of the early Roman Empire, but this technique flourished during the 3rd and 4th centuries (Cermanović-Kuzmanović 1976, 175–190). It consists of casting in a mould and the insertion of foil shaped in the form of medallions. At first, these gold leaves were decorated with mythological scenes, and in Late Antiquity, Christian motifs also appeared. Along with the inscriptions, we often also find the Christogram with the apocalyptic letters α and ω.[48]

The majority of finds with family presentations originate from the West, although it is believed that the origin of this technique is eastern. Most were found in Italy, and a considerable number of these finds are recorded in Pannonia (Migotti 2003, 15).[49] Therefore, it is a common

Figure 4.2. Prahovo–*Aquae*. Gilded glass base. (Documentation of the National Museum of Serbia).

opinion among scholars that the largest production centre for gilded glass bases was Rome (Miggoti 2003, 16). There is also an assumption that Trier might have been the second important production centre of glass bases

---

[47] The gilded glass base came to the National Museum in Belgrade through a purchase in 1977 (inv. no. 1511/IV). According to uncertain data given by the owner, a cross-shaped fibula (inv. no. 1519/IV), which will be discussed later, was found together with this base.

[48] More about decoration of these finding see: Ilić, Jeremić 2018, 268.

[49] Until now, about 500 pieces of gilded glass bases made in the *fondi d'oro* technique with engraved depictions have been found in the territory of the entire empire. Apart from Rome and Italy, gilded glass bases, though small in number, were evidenced in: Austria, Germany, France, Spain, Hungary, Bulgaria, Serbia, Croatia, and Slovenia. In the province of Pannonia, there are as many as four out of five found specimens with presentations of married couples, in provincial production: two originate from Štrbinci near Đakovo in Croatia, and two are from Hungary.

made in the *fondi d'oro* technique (Cambi 1976, 141). On the other hand, there is an opposite opinion according to which all these items were manufactured in the east, Egypt or Syria (Cermanović-Kuzmanović 1976, 180). The find from *Aquae* can be dated to the 4th century, taking into consideration numerous analogies, primarily from the province of Pannonia (Migotti 2003, sl. 3. 5, 6, 10, 12, 15, 16).

The question of the purpose of these gilded glass bases made using the *fondi d'oro* technique is still not completely resolved. A considerable number were parts of grave goods. It is an interesting fact that in most cases only the bases of the vessels have been found and never a whole vessel. According to some authors, glass vessels with gilded bases were ritually broken on the grave of the buried (Migotti 2003, 16–17). A plausible original function of these finds could only be discussed based on preserved whole vessels or depictions that could clearly determine the purpose of the vessel.

5

Church Inventory

The illumination of a space played an important role in different cultures and religions. In numerous theories, the creation of light occupies a special place in mythologies (*Genesis*, 1, 3). The relationship with light had an uninterrupted tradition since Antiquity, both in terms of its use in profane buildings, but also in sacral architecture. Christianity took on the use of light, not only for practical, but especially for religious and symbolic reasons, by observing the liturgical practices from the Old Testament.[50] Light became one of the fundamental symbols of Christianity. Its nature was linked to the presence of the Divine power in the material world. By following the symbolism established in the Old Testament, light became a positive symbol in the New Testament as well, representing God, and God revealed through an identification with Christ, who says of himself: "I am the light of the world and whoever follows me will not walk in darkness, but will have the light of life" (John 8, 12).

The most direct illustration of the importance of light in early Christian theology is Nicene Creed, or the "symbol of faith", according to which Jesus Christ was equal to Lord, His Father. The Biblical symbolic language of light became part of texts, hymns and liturgies of the Holy Fathers, who proclaimed the Divine presence in light. Thus, through *Christus Sol*, early Christianity marked, in a way, the transition from the worship of *Sol Invictus* to the worship of *Christus Verus Sol*. Unlike the pagan cults, which worshiped sunlight and the astral Sun as a god, it was in this manner that Christ stepped out, with his incarnation as the only True Sun – *Christus Verus*, who brings the light of enlightenment and salvation. Making Christ and the Sun to be one and the same was a means to suppress the pagan cults by accepting them in a new, Christian sense. The language of Clement of Alexandria refers to the Divine Light that the believers put on as a garment at their baptism: Christ is the True and Eternal Light (Clem. *Paedag*. II, X, 207; XI, 244).

Paulinus of Nola, in one of his poems, says that Christ is equal to the Sun – *Sol aequitatis*, the truest light – *veritatis lumen est* and the true Apollo (Paulini, *Poem* X, 25, 50). For the Holy Fathers of the Church, the question of the distinction between the two terms, *lux* and *lumen,* was also exceptionally important, with *lux* being a translation of the Greek φῶς, referring to the light of the Genesis and to Christ, while *lumen* represented a derivative from the Greek word λύχνος, signifying light from a physical source, like a lamp or a candle (Cabrol et Leclercq 1921, 1726).[51] This topic was separately deepened, almost at the same time, by Saint Augustine in the West and the Cappadocian Fathers in the East, whose theology was close to Neo–Platonism. Saint Augustine makes a distinction between the primary Divine Light – *lux*, and the light provided by celestial bodies – *luminaria*, but he believes that both these lights are necessary in order to achieve enlightenment (Aug. *Genesi.* XI, 23).

5.1. Polycandela

The tendency of multiplying light sources led to the creation of polycandela. It is believed that they began to be used more widely only at some point in the 4th century, when Christianity became the official religion and people could freely attend liturgies. Considering the great need for these items, an increasingly larger number of polycandela that used to be made from precious metals would be replaced, in time, with less expensive, most commonly, bronze lamps.

The prototype for polycandela should be sought in Antique lamps, in which we encounter the basic elements of polycandela, such as ring-shaped pottery oil lamps with radially distributed holes for wicks, or lamps in the shape of a basilica, with protruding handles in the shape of the bodies of dolphins, ending with ring-shaped holes for lamps (Cabrol et Leclercq 1928, 6742/12). Polycandela developed from simple metal hoops, on which candles were radially distributed. In time, candles would be replaced with vessels containing oil, which provided more durable illumination of higher quality (Mirković 1965, 321).[52] The large number of findings of polycandela indicates that they were widely present in the entire Empire, due to the already mentioned need for the permanent lighting of the church area.[53]

The simplest forms of polycandela consisted of perforated stands, which could have been in the shape of a circle, polygonal or in the shape of a cross, in which glass lamps would be placed (Baumstark, ed. 1998, cat. 93, 95, 96). Gradually, polycandela of simple forms, adapted to their basic function, would become richly decorated chandeliers

---

[50] In Jewish liturgy, the eternal flame burned before the altar, in the vestibule (Lev. 6, 6). The light which was thus constantly burning was the symbol of God himself.

[51] The word λύχνος is a Greek term used in the meaning "lamp", and in the metaphorical language of the patristics, John the Baptist is λύχνος, because while he himself is not the "light", he came to bear witness to the "light", φῶς (John, 1, 7–8).

[52] Starting from the 4th century, wax and olive oil began to be used as materials for illumination during liturgical rites, since they had a certain symbolism in Christianity.

[53] As parts of the church inventory, polycandela and lamps made of precious metals and bronze represent items that are the most common elements of church hoards discovered today.

of the great churches of Rome, Constantinople, Cairo and Jerusalem, whose opulence and elegance are known from their descriptions in numerous historical sources. Thus, at the end of the 4th and the beginning of the 5th century, *Liber Pontificalis* mentions a whole series of gifts that Constantine the Great gave to the Lateran Church. Among other items, a chandelier stands out with 4 crowns and 20 dolphins made of pure gold, "*et farum ex auro purissimo qui pendit sub fastidium cum delfinos L ex auro purissimo, pens. lib. L.*" (*Lib. Pont.* XXXIIII, SIL. 9).[54]

The most luxurious lamps were called *coronae* or *coronae farales*. Next are the somewhat less lavish examples, known as *fara (phara) canthara* and *gabat(h)ae* (Chevalier 1999, 162). Judging by the description, items made of gold were grouped in the eastern part of the church. Thus, *coronae* made of gold were hung in front of the altar and under the *ciborium* – *sub fastigium*, one in the centre and four under the arches of the *ciborium*. In the main nave, 45 silver polycandela and silver lamps (*fara argentea*) were placed along the lateral naves, while there were 50 silver candelabra at the centre of the basilica, illuminating the inside of the church and, at the same time, contributing to the general image of richness and opulence (*Lib. Pont.* XXXIIII, SIL. 11). By placing the gold items in the eastern part, and the silver ones in the central and western parts, the hierarchy of the space was stressed. Naturally, precious metals were most commonly used in the mobiliary of imperial foundations and they were not a part of the inventory of every church.

The richness and splendour of polycandela that adorned the Church of Saint Sophia in Constantinople in the 6th century were witnessed by Paulus Silentiarius (Cabrol et Leclercq 1939, 1356). He mentions large polycandela in circular and cross-shaped forms, hung by chains from the dome of the church, above the heads of the faithful. An especially impressive example was the polyeleos lamp under the dome made of silver, with crystal censers that resembled a crown once they were lit up. The lamps were grouped in certain places, which probably contributed to a general visual impression of richness and splendour. Thus, a circle of lamps was placed near the bottom of the dome, leaning onto the fence of the *cancella*, while others hung from the walls or colonnades that separated the naves of the church. Remains of such luxurious examples, whose descriptions are provided by historical sources, have not been found as yet. We may assume that their opulence and the precious metals from which they were made are the reason they have not been preserved. Polycandela that we can find in museum collections in our country and worldwide today represent more modest, mostly bronze, examples. A rare find of a silver polycandelon represents a part of the Lampsacus Treasure (Hellespont), which is now housed at the British Museum (Dalton 1901, 85, cat. 393).

According to the production type, that is to say, according to their shapes, polycandela have been classified into two basic types. The first type comprehends those with a hanging metal hoop, with protruding handles that served as supports for glass or pottery oil-lamps. The second type would comprehend polyeleos lamps in a circular shape, made in the *opus interrasile* technique, by means of which numerous holes for censers were made. On the basis of the holes for censers as well as handles in the first type of polyeleos lamps, there are numerous names for this type of church inventory: polyeleos lamp, polycandelon, *corona lucis*. Polycandela were placed on fixed supports. They usually consist of bronze wires, lamellas or hanging chains, ending with a hook, which were hung from the ceiling, dome or walls. Their arms also ended with smaller hooks, which were used directly to support the censers. Often, a cross or a medallion would appear as an element of the supports, pierced through at the top and the bottom and linked to the supports. Lamps that were parts of polycandela were inserted in ring-shaped holes. They were most commonly made of glass, although there are also pottery lamps, as was the case with those originating from St. Peter's Church in Jerusalem (Cabrol et Leclercq 1939, 1356–1357). From *Romuliana* originates several fragments of glass lamps, parts of polycandela that were inserted in holes (Fig. 5.1). Aside from glass and baked clay, metal was also used for the making of censers, like examples from the Vasilevski Collection, where oil lamps with mobile lids, in the shape of doves, had the function of censers (Cabrol et Leclercq 1924, 4767).

The question of the origin and production of Early Christian polycandela has not been precisely determined as yet. The largest number of examples discovered so far come from the Christian East and North Africa. Even though they are typical of Coptic churches, their production cannot be linked only to this territory, that is to say, to Egypt, but the wider Mediterranean region instead.

The polycandelon from *Romuliana* represents a part of a hoard of church items, which comprehended, aside from this polycandelon: a hexagonal censer, a candelabrum and mushroom-shaped fittings (Fig. 3.6a) (Janković 1983, 135, sl. 178–180; Živić 2003, 71, sl. 30). All the items were made of bronze and discovered in a tower of the older fortification. These items were most probably put aside at the end of the 6th century, during a period of common Avar–Slav attacks in the territory of the Empire. Its simplicity of production can be seen in the omission of any decorative details, with only the functional elements kept, therefore, it represents a more modest example of a polycandelon, with simplified or completely omitted decorative elements. The closest parallel is an example kept at the Benaki Museum in Athens (Duval et Jeremić 1984, 133, fig. 130c). Based on their simplicity, two bronze examples from the collection of the Louvre are close to the example from *Romuliana*; they also consist of a metal hoop

---

[54] It was calculated that one donation of Constantine to the Lateran Basilica in Rome consisted of 169 lighting bodies with 8730 individual lamps, which is the best illustration of the importance of these parts of the church inventory: *cf.* Cabrol et Leclercq, Eclairage des *églises* 1921, 1726–1730.

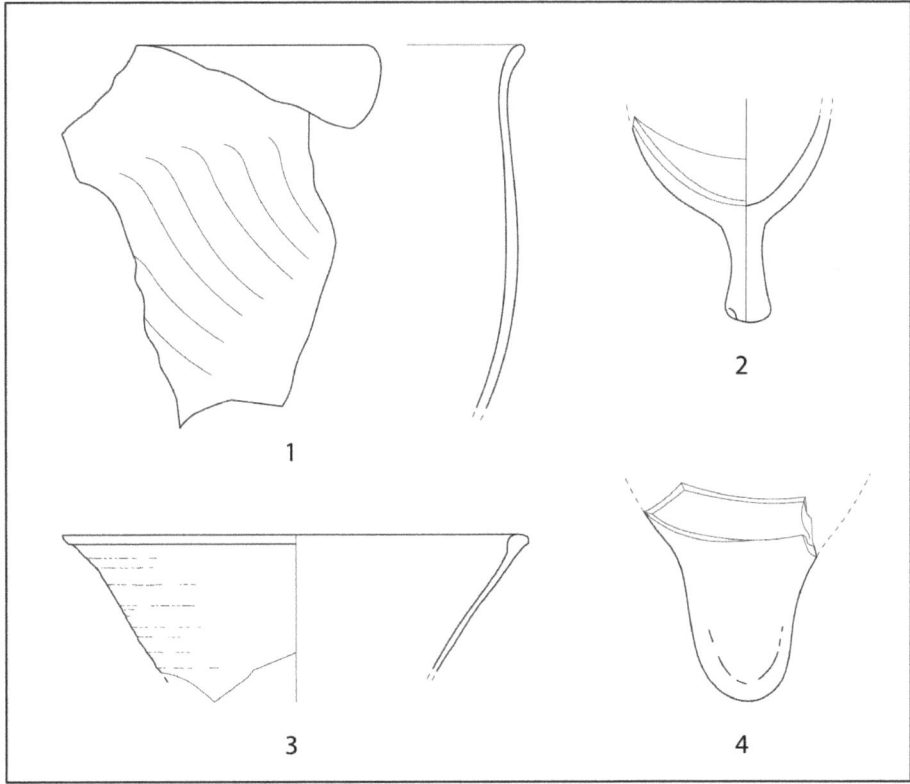

Figure 5.1. Gamzigrad–*Romuliana*. Glass lamps – parts of polycandela.

with holes for censers, and made in the *opus interrasile* technique (Bénazeth 1992, 164–165, E13524, 11916, 6). They most probably represent Coptic products from the 6th and 7th century. Another similar finding, but with a cross in the middle and holes for six lamps, comes from an unknown site and represents a part of the private "Wolf Family" collection in Jerusalem (Israeli and Mevorah, eds. 2000, 108). The polycandelon from *Romuliana* can be linked to the activity of the Early Christian church in the area of the central Balkans. Its simplicity of production compared to the model it was based on indicates that it was most probably a product of local workshops, where the craftsman was not skilful enough, and he did have a model of a polyeleos lamp before him that was made in one of the more important workshop centres.

5.2. Candelabra

Among the items that represented parts of the church inventory, a special place is held by candelabra. The need for lamps that could be placed freely in the space led to the creation of candelabra, whose form is reminiscent of architectonic shapes with bases, entases and capitals. Candelabra became a part of the Christian inventory, especially from the 4th century, when they began to be used in churches during liturgical rites, but also during funerary rites. Christian iconography often depicts candelabra with candles that illuminate the relics of saints or martyrs.[55]

As a part of the Christian ritual, candelabra increasingly replaced lamps when it comes to illumination, keeping this function up to today. Among the numerous presents that Constantine the Great gave to the Lateran Church, which we have already mentioned, luxurious candelabra made of silver and orichalcum are also listed (Cabrol 1910, 1834–1835).

So far, only one candelabrum has been discovered in the territory of the Roman Danube Valley provinces, originating from the already mentioned hoard from *Romuliana* (Janković 1983, 135, kat. 179; Živić 2003, 70–71, sl. 30). The stand of the candelabra is in the shape of a tripod, with ends in the form of dolphins and stylised leaves of a grapevine between the arms (Fig. 3.6b). The trunk is fluted, and the recipient is in the shape of a stylised flower, with a spike for the candle at the centre. Christian symbolism on this example is present in the form of the representation of dolphins.

Examples analogous to our candelabrum, originating from the Christian East, most prominently Egypt and Syria, kept in the Dumbarton Oaks Collection in Washington (Ross 1962, 33, 39, Pl. XVII, XIX). A silver candelabrum from Syria (the hoard from Hama) should also be mentioned, kept at the Walters Art Gallery in Baltimore today (Mundell-Mango 1986, 96–98, cat. 11). All the listed examples are chronologically determined into the 6th century. According

---

[55] Lighted candles used in the cult of a saint or during the burial of a believer were not merely intended for paying respects, but also to indicate the idea of joy and eternity, which accompany the soul on its journey from earthly to eternal life.

to its stylistic traits, the find from *Romuliana* can also be dated into that same period.

Candelabra were made in certain production centres, from which they reached different parts of the Empire via trade. Those were most prominently centres in Christian Egypt, where the Copts developed a high level of craft production that was characterised not only by high precision, but also by the beauty of shape and decorative content. We can assume for the finding from *Romuliana* that it was produced in one of the crafts centres in the Christian East and that it was imported to *Romuliana*, which could have already been a larger ecclesiastic seat for the area of the province of *Dacia Ripensis* in the 6th century, as shown by the preserved remains of sacral architecture within the fortification (Čanak-Medić 1978, 127–140; Janković 1983, 120–130; Petković 2010, 196–199, sl. 170). It can be noted that candelabra from the 6th century represent simplified variations compared to the examples from the 4th and the 5th century (Ross 1962, cat. 33, 38, 39, 40, Pl. XXVII, XXVIII, XXIX). The changes can be seen, first and foremost, in the shaping of the upper part of the candelabrum, which was completely adapted for placing candles at that point.

5.3. Lamps

The art of casting bronze items, inherited from the Antique times, continued in the period of the Roman Empire, which had already been Christianised at that point, in the 4th century. Among those items, an important place was taken by lamps. Different possibilities in the production of lamps became prominent, both in terms of the manner of production and in the artistic expression, and that can be noted not only in those lamps used in a liturgical context but also in those intended for profane contexts. Lamps used in liturgical practice continued the Antique tradition in terms of their form, with decorative motifs mostly indicating their Christian character. During liturgical rites, which were performed at night and underground at the beginning, it was necessary to have suitable lighting. Lamps were also lit on the graves of Christian martyrs, the light of the lamps personifying the light of the word of God. Along with the religious character, lamps also had a profane character. Aside from private houses, they were also used to illuminate streets, public buildings, *thermae* and squares. The material from which they were made would actually influence their application. Bronze lamps were used for liturgical rites or to illuminate sacral buildings, while pottery lamps were used more for the illumination of graves or for domestic use.

Lamps were made from metal, most commonly bronze, baked clay or glass. Most were made of clay, while the bronze ones were considered to be more luxurious items, and they were often melted down, therefore, they are preserved in smaller numbers compared to those made of baked clay. As for the processing technique of bronze lamps, they were cast and chiselled, the same as most bronze items in applied arts. Based on their manner of placement, they can be divided into: hanging, standing and hand lamps, factors that largely determined their shape and decoration (Kaufman 1913, 608).

During the 3rd century, a notable delay in the production of lamps, as well as a decrease in the production quality, can be noted in the territory of the Roman Empire. Apparently, it was the consequence of a general crisis in society, but also of an interruption in the organised distribution of lamps, which led to the creation of a larger number of local production centres.[56] In the 4th century, along with the rise of Christianity, a new expansion in the production of lamps occurred and those with a Christian message and content became ever more numerous.

The themes on Christian lamps were most commonly scenes from the Old Testament, motifs from the life of Christ, figures of saints, as well as Christian symbols. The depiction of a cross or a Christogram was an especially favoured motif on lamps from the Early Christian period. As with Antique lamps, Christian ones were also made in the shape of a boat (*navicella*), with one or more holes for the wick, and a handle located at the stern (*acrostolium*). At some point, starting from the 4th century, handles on bronze lamps began to be decorated with Christ's monogram (Tatić-Đurić 1960, 240).

By observing the history of the use of lamps, it can be noted that there was a specialisation of sorts from the earliest times, that is to say, that lamps intended for cult contexts or residential buildings were of higher quality, often from higher quality metals and more expensive, of larger dimensions and with more burners. During the Late Antiquity, due to a series of factors, these differences became increasingly more prominent, hence, at the beginning of the 6th century, there was a great change in the quality and quantity of lighting equipment used in sacral buildings compared to those used in everyday life. While interiors of churches were equipped with lavish polyeleos lamps, candelabra and lamps made of precious metals, the lighting for homes became increasingly more modest, reverting to archaic forms (Bouras and Parani 2009, 27).

In Late Antiquity, on a wider scale, lamps of higher quality and with rich decorations were produced from the 4th up to the 7th century in the area of Asia Minor to North Africa, from where they were exported all over the Mediterranean, to large ports in Constantinople, Thessaloniki, Aquileia and other coastal centres, from where some examples reached the inner parts of the European continent by land (Ilić 2011, 40–41).

The research of lamps in cult contexts shows that their symbolical value is that of vessels of light, by their function and place in a given ritual: as an object which

---

[56] Even though lamps, especially pottery lamps, represented relatively cheap items, their transport would significantly increase their price. It is not surprising, therefore, that the influence of local production would increase in times of crises, such as the 3rd century, when interruptions occured in the Roman system of the transport of goods.

Figure 5.2. Panjevac near Ćuprija. A bronze lamp with the handle in the shape of the head of a griffin. (Documentation of the National Museum of Serbia).

provides light, a vessel that contains consecrated oil in the cult of a saint or reliquaries. The decoration was not crucial for the symbolic or practical role of a lamp. Regardless of that, it can be noted that decorations changed depending on the religious and social circumstances. Late Antique lamps show notable variations in shape and typology, a consequence of a long tradition of production and use, which was manifested in a transformation of standard types, as well as a large number of local workshops that appeared in the Mediterranean region from the 2nd century and took precedence in the production of lamps during the 3rd century.[57]

Bronze lamps

A bronze lamp in the shape of a griffin represents a part of the Collection of the National Museum in Belgrade. It originates from the area of the Roman province of *Moesia Prima*, from the site of Panjevac, near Ćuprija. The lamp is distinctive by its handle, in the shape of the head of a griffin (Jeličić 1959, 79; Kondić 1993, 337, cat. 145; Ilić 2011, 39, fig. 12/2; Cvjetićanin 2013, 215, kat. 166). It belongs to the type of hanging lamps, with two holes: one for the oil, the other for the wick (Fig. 5.2). The body of the lamp is round, with a fleur-de-lis motif on both ends. In the middle of the body, on both sides, there is a Christogram. The hole for the oil is placed on the top of the body, and it used to have a lid, which is lost today. There is a decorative ring, with transverse carved lines at the transition point from the body of the lamp to the handle and the nozzle. The elongated nozzle ends in the shape of a flower with nine petals, with a wick hole at the centre. The handle is shaped in the form of the head of a griffin. The mane is depicted with three triangular outgrowths on the neck, ending with droplets. The head was precisely modelled, with a bent nozzle, and with a droplet. There is a Christogram at the top of the head, with a dove on it. The foot of the lamp is small and ring-shaped. The hoop intended for the hanging of the lamp was preserved on the head and the body of the griffin.

A zoomorphic handle in the form of a griffin's head was present on a series of analogous examples, discovered across the entire Mediterranean area (Italy, Egypt, Syria). They are mostly dated into the period from the 4th to the 6th century. The Christian symbolism on a lamp kept at the Vatican Museum is similar to the one on our lamp. It has an elongated shape, symbolising a boat, whose

---

[57] On the typological analysis of Roman and Late Antique pottery lamps from *Viminacium*: cf. Korać, M. *Oil lamps from Viminacium – Moesia Superior*, Beograd 2018.

stern ends in the shape of a griffin's head, which has a monogram cross with a dove above it, and an apple in the mouth (Tatić-Đurić 1960, 242). Lamps of this type can be made in a completely simple manner, from those without the presence of any symbols, up to the lamps with exquisitely artistically worked details, both of the head of the griffin and the Christian symbols as well. Among such examples, a lamp kept at the Virginia Museum of Fine Arts, in Richmond should be especially singled out (Gonosová and Kondoleon 1994, cat. 85). It is dated into the period from the 4th to the 6th century. A lamp that most probably originated from Constantinople, and which is kept at the Munich Collection, also belongs to this group (Stiegemann Ch., ed. 2001, II/6). Unlike our lamp, this one has two wick holes. A monogram cross with the apocalyptic letters α and ω is present on the lamp. It belongs to the hanging lamps type. It is dated into the 4th–5th century. A lamp similar to the find from Panjevac comes from the British Museum, which has a chain with a hanging hook preserved, confirming that, in this case, it was a hanging lamp (Dalton 1901, cat. 502, Pl. XXVII). There are slight differences in the actual shaping of the head and the neck of the griffin. Chronologically it belongs to the period from the 5th to the 7th century.

Another lamp of a similar shape, with a handle in the shape of a griffin's head, is kept at the Dumbarton Oaks Collection (Ross 1962, cat. 30, pl. XXV). The oil lid was in the form of a shell, which is reminiscent of a lamp example from the Belgrade City Museum, which has an identical lid. It originates from Constantinople, and it is dated into the 4th–5th century.

For all these lamps, rich zoomorphic and vegetable ornaments are typical, especially in the decoration of the handles. The present combination of a griffin with Christian symbols cannot be linked to the adoption of this pagan symbol by the Christian church. The presence of Christian symbols on lamps of this type made them acceptable for Christian use, either for cult purposes, or for domestic use. It would appear that the presence of a griffin on the lamps was a short-lived fashion, coming from the merger of this Antique mythical creature with Christian symbols. The manner in which this pagan motif was incorporated into the Christian iconography and completely Christianised is especially interesting. In Greek mythology, griffins are mythical quadrupeds with the body of a lion, head of an eagle and eyes blazing with fire. They were primarily a symbol of Apollo, but they were occasionally linked to Artemis and Dionysus. Since they combine the strength of the lion and the power of the eagle, they were symbols of divine strength and constant vigilance. They were also considered to be the protectors of graves, hence, they often appeared in funerary art (Srejović and Cermanović-Kuzmanović 1992, 99). In the first centuries of Christianity, a new challenge presented itself before its theology: how to reconcile the Christian worldview with the habits of Antique man. In order to avoid an unacceptable connection to the pagan god of light, but also healing, the apotropaic symbol of the griffin was Christianised and subordinated to Christ's true light, which was stressed with Christ's monogram being depicted twice on the body of the lamp.[58] The relationship between Christ and Apollo was a topic that interested Early Christian writers as well. In his *Poem X*, Paulinus of Nola speaks of Christ as the only *Verus Sol*; the enlightenment he represents leads to salvation and brings new life, while only the ignorant address Apollo Phoebus and the muses (Paulini, *Poem* X, 25, 50). Through the representation of a griffin with a Christogram on its head, with the Christian symbol of a dove on it, *Christus Verus* triumphs over Apollo.

From all this, we can conclude that the decorative repertoire of the lamp brings together the pagan and the Christian symbols in the spirit of the syncretism of Late Antiquity. The popularity of this type of lamp was confirmed with the large number of preserved examples, bearing witness of the fact that bringing pagan and Christian motifs together was acceptable for the people of Late Antiquity who did not renounce their old protectors and magic practices easily. According to the stylistic traits of the lamp, i.e. the combination of Late Antique craftsmanship, where the technique and the form kept the elements of the Antique heritage, and the presence of Christian symbolism, reflected in the presence of the monogram cross, dove, and an apple in the mouth of the griffin, we can chronologically determine the finding from Panjevac into the Late Antique period, i.e. in the period of the 4th–5th century.

A bronze lamp with a cover in the form of a shell and an elongated beak, together with a cast cruciform handle, originates from *Singidunum* (5.3) (Ilić, Jeremić 2918, 260–261 fig. 7; Janković 2007, 312).[59] Bronze lamps similar to our specimen usually had mounting equipment, chains used for hanging or a stand, which has not been preserved on the lamp from *Singidunum*. This type of lamp was found in different areas of the Late Antiquity and represents part of the collections of many museums and private collections. Close analogies originate from the immediate surroundings, from Stobi in North Macedonia (Grupa autora 1980, kat. 555) and the Luciu site in Romania (Teodor 2001, 119, fig. 5/2). In the Bode Museum (Kaiser Friedrich Museum) in Berlin, there is a similar lamp with a preserved stand.[60] In the Louvre, in the Egyptian collection, similar specimens are also to be found (Bénazeth 1992, 122–123, E11924, E142839).

In the period of Late Antiquity, the most important bronze lamp production centres were in the Eastern Mediterranean, and they were particularly mass-produced in Egypt, where they were most likely products of Coptic workshops, in

---

[58] Christians showed antagonism towards pagan gods with healing powers, such as Apollo or Asclepius. That made them similar to Christ, thus bringing his uniqueness into question.
[59] There is no precise data about the finding place of the lamp, except that it was found in the area of Belgrade. It is housed in the Collection of the Migration Period and the Middle Ages, in the Belgrade City Museum.
[60] During a visit to the Bode Museum, the author took a photograph of the lamp.

Church Inventory

Figure 5.3. Belgrade–*Singidunum*. Bronze lamp with a cross-like handle. (Documentation of the Belgrade City Museum).

the period from the 5th to the 7th century, from where they were distributed throughout the Roman empire (Nesbitt 1988, no. 26–31).

As with certain Antique examples, there were also Christian lamps made in the shape of a boat (*navicella*), with one or more wick holes, and a handle placed at the stern (*acrostolium*). One such finding comes from Smederevo, from the site of Mezul (*Vinceia*). It is a ten-wick lamp in the shape of a boat, cast in bronze (Figs. 5.4; 5.5). A part of the boat's stern was elongated with a representation of a fantastic beast in the form of a dragon (*draco*), ornamentally shaped, holding a human Fig. in its jaws, which reminds us, at first glance, of the story of Jonah. The sea fauna on the sides of the boat, the content of which corresponds to the main motif, symbolises the sea, all the temptations and torments through which a ship must sail. The central place is taken by representations of dolphins, as one of the most important Early Christian symbols. Today, the lamp is missing its lid (the deck), the mast of the ship and most probably human figures, placed on the deck. There is a votive inscription on the prow and the stern, and it can be read and interpreted in two ways:

dei – in domu – Termogenes – votum fecit – which would indicate more of a pagan character, or: *in domu – dei – Termogenes – votum fecit*, which would reveal a more Jewish or Christian sense (Popović 1970, 324). *Domus dei* is an expression most commonly denominating a Jewish temple in the Old Testament, but it could also possibly refer to a house in which Christians would gather. In the New Testament, it could comprehend the Christian community in general. During the times when Christianity became the official religion, church edifices were denominated with terms: *ecclesia*, *basilica*, and more rarely with *domus dei*. The second part of the inscription, *Termogenes votum fecit*, does not provide an actual answer to the question of the bearer of the name. It most probably refers to the person who ordered the lamp, and not the craftsman who made it. When it comes to the dedicant of this lamp, *Termogenes*, some authors believe that the lack of *tria nomina* would

Figure 5.4. Smederevo (Mezul)–*Vinceia*. Bronze lamp in the form of a ship (Documentation of the Museum in Smederevo).

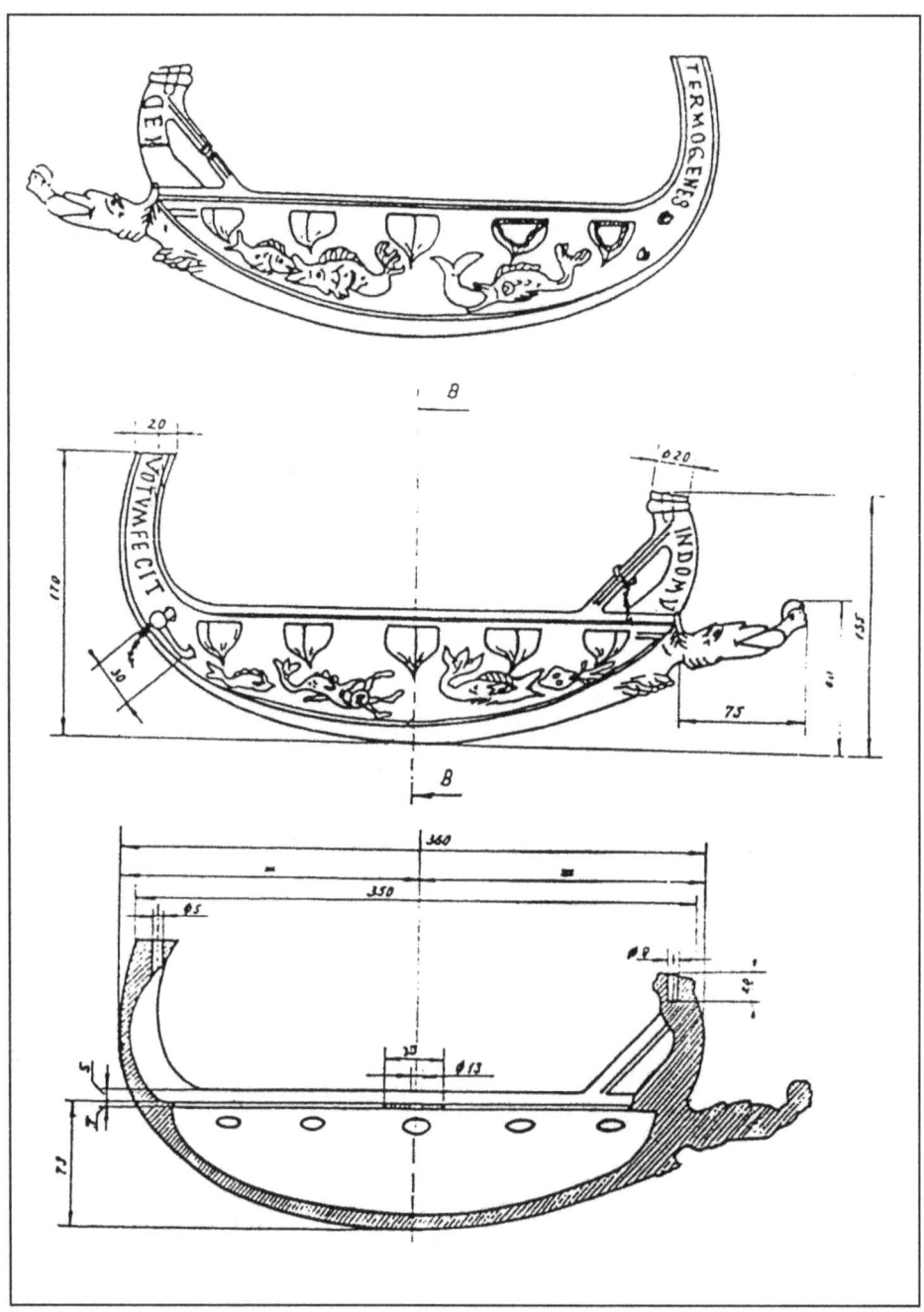

Figure 5.5. Smederevo, Mezul site–*Vinceia*. Bronze lamp in the form of ship.

suggest his Greek origin. This is indicated not only by the Greek shape of the boat, but also the Greek name of the person who ordered it, for which the translation "born in *thermae*" is suggested (Pavlović 1967, 126). *Termogenes* could have been baptised in *thermae*, and not in a baptistery intended for this ceremony, which would indicate that this lamp could have been made before the 313 AD.

When it comes to the symbolism of the lamp, most authors agree in their analyses that the representations of sea fauna, dolphins swallowing cephalopods, and a dragon with a human in its jaws, depict a personified battle of good versus evil (Pavlović 1967, 127–128). This dualism exists in many religions, Christianity among others as well. Next, we can also note a symbolically depicted concept of the migration of souls. The boat transporting human souls also has a symbolism of its own. In Christian iconography, a boat and a dove shown together represent the journey of a soul towards Heaven. Good and evil spirits are shown fighting around the soul. They would be greeted by Oranta on Paradise Island. All these philosophical and theological teachings of the Antique society were accepted and adapted by Christianity for its own ideology. However, the lamp is missing the mast with sails, which used to exist, as one of the important elements of Christian symbolism. Namely, Christian Fathers from the 2nd and the 3rd century considered the boat to be a symbol of the church, leading across tempestuous waves to the *portus salutis*. The mast with sails symbolised the cross – *antenna crucis*.

A part of the prow is elongated, with the representation of a fantastic beast, ornamentally made, holding a man in its jaws, and reminding of the event with Jonah, who, in turn, is a symbolic representation of Christ's passion and resurrection. As with Jonah, who spent three days and three nights in the belly of a sea monster, according to the story from the Old Testament, Christ also spent three days and three nights in the ground (Matthew 12, 40). This was a favourite topic of Early Christian mosaics and sarcophagi of the 4th century, and we can see it on the sarcophagus from Belgrade as well.[61]

The Book of Jonah is most commonly illustrated through several episodes: Jonah being cast into the sea from the ship, Jonah being swallowed and then vomited out by the sea creature, and Jonah reposing in the shade of a gourd. In this manner, a symbolic depiction is given of the sacrifice of Jonah, his earthly grave and Paradise. Those representations were reduced to only those parts of the story that give the central message, with everything superfluous omitted (Valtrović 1891a, 130–142; Pilipović and Milanović 2016, 219–245). Sometimes, only one scene is depicted, most commonly Jonah in the gourd shade. In the case of the lamp from Mezul, the moment was depicted – adapted to the shape of the boat on which it is shown – when the sea monster vomits Jonah out onto the land, that is to say, the moment of salvation, corresponding to the meaning of the ship. The sea fauna on the sides of the boat, whose contents corresponds to the main motif, symbolises the sea, all the temptations and dangers through which a ship has to sail. Namely, the fight of the dolphins is symbolically given in the moment when they swallow cephalopods, thus symbolising the dualism of good and evil.

There are few analogies for this type of lamp. It most probably comes from the period of the Empire and it indicates a connection to Rome, considering the fact that a similar lamp was discovered in Rome, in the ruins of the palace of Emperor Valentinian (254–260 AD), and is kept at the Archaeological Museum in Florence today (Brenk 2003, fig. 187; Kaufman 1913, 295–296). The text on this lamp is written on a plaque at the top of the mast. This example was hanging from wire hoops, and it has only two fire holes on the sides, differing from our example. Hoops in a figure-of-eight shape were also used here, at the prow and the stern, and gathered in a ring, from which the lamp hung.

A common trait of both these lamps is that they are in the shape of a boat. It should be mentioned that a bent bronze wire ring was preserved on both the prow and the stern of the lamp from Mezul. Three figure-of-eight hoops were preserved on the ring at the prow, which could indicate that this was a hanging lamp. Judging by the human figures on the Florentine example, one of the authors who analysed the lamp assumed that the same figures existed on the example from Mezul as well (Pavlović 1967, 127–128). One could have been placed at the prow of the boat, and another one probably also on the missing deck of the boat (the lid). We cannot determine for certain where the lamp was made. An assumption was made that it could have originated from Campania.

When it comes to the dating of this lamp, unique in this territory, opinions of various authors differ. According to L. Pavlović, the lamp could have been made in the times of Hadrian (117–138 AD), an emperor who was fond of the Greeks, and Greek culture and cults (Pavlović 1967, 128). On the basis of the ambiguous formulation of the inscription, which we have already mentioned, as well as the palaeographic traits of the inscription, V. Popović believes that this example should be dated into the 3rd century (Popović 1970, 329). What we can say with certainty is that this lamp has a votive character, clearly indicated by the inscription, on which the gift-giver was noted by his name.

The lamp is one of the most representative preserved Late Antique lamps of this form. It is, however, difficult to explain this unique find and to determine to whom it belonged, to a Christian community or to an individual, but it was most probably the property of a member of the Christian faith and it represents an example of the early presence of Christianity in the territory of *Moesia Prima*. According to the already mentioned analogous lamp from Florence, we can also chronologically determine this example into the second half of the 3rd or the beginning of the 4th century.

In accordance with the suggestion by V. Popović that the lamp was discovered *in situ*, in a place where a Roman *villa rustica* was located, the possibility should be taken into consideration that, at some point, the villa was turned into a house church – *domus dei*. The building could have been linked to the nearby Roman city of *Vinceia*, where epigraphic and archaeological evidence was found of the existence of an Eastern and Christian community. A statuette of the Good Shepherd and a lead sarcophagus with a cross were discovered in the vicinity. The numerous questions that remain unanswered for the time being could be resolved with a systematic research of the site. The considered hypotheses remain only hypothetical. Regardless of whether they are well founded or not, they do illustrate the amount of data that can be obtained from a seemingly simple object, primarily intended for everyday use, such as a lamp.

Pottery lamps

Pottery lamps are represented by several examples in the Danube provinces of *Moesia Prima* and *Dacia Ripensis*. The Early Christian motifs on pottery lamps appear on both local and on imported types of lamps. It can be assumed that such lamps had an important place in the lives of Christians in the Late Antique period, as

---
[61] More about the sarcophagus from *Singidunum* in the next chapter.

Figure 5.6. Belgrade–*Singidunum*. Pottery lamp with two figures and crosses. (Documentation of the Belgrade City Museum).

votive offerings, or in the sphere of private piety, where they were used in homes, during prayer, but also in the funerary cult. Judging by the small number of imported, but also local lamps, with specifically Christian themes in the overall number of preserved lamps from the wider area of the Central Balkans, lamps that were decorated with motifs which are not strictly Christian – such as rosettes, geometrical ornaments or motifs of fish, dolphins, deer, kantharos, grapevine with grapes, etc. seem to have been acceptable for the votive lighting of lamps in churches, or for being placed in graves. Unfortunately, the current research level of Early Christian sites and insufficiently researched finding contexts in the past do not allow for more reliable conclusions.

A pottery lamp with Christian symbols on it comes from *Singidunum*. The lamp has an oval shape with a ring handle and an elongated beak (Fig. 5.6).[62] The disc is round and rimmed with a ring made of plastic dots. Two figures, male and female, in an orant position, are presented on the disc. Besides this depiction there are crosses on the disc, the beak and a third one on the leg of the lamp. All three crosses are made of relief dots (Ilić, Jeremić 2018, 274).

The lamp from the Belgrade City Museum has been published several times, but without exact provenance, with the remark that it shows Eastern influences, but that it is probably local work (Birtašević 1955, 43–46; Birtašević 1970, 7–8; Janković 2000, 29–30). D. Tešić-Radovanović expressed the opposite opinion based on analogies from Athens and Florence, all three lamps belong to the circle of pilgrimage items related to the cult of the Holy Mina, which were produced near Abu Mena, but also in other craft centres of Egypt, such as Antinopolis. Lamps of this type were made from the middle of the 5th century, until the Arab conquest of Antinopolis 641 AD, after which production was stopped, and the city experienced stagnation and began to decline (Tešić-Radovanović 2018, 173–174). The appearance of this lamp in the Balkans suggests that it did not reach this area through trade, but most likely as a pilgrimage item.

The other finds originating from the Danube provinces of the Central Balkans are mostly represented by lamps of an oval form with a cross in combination with floral and geometric ornament as a dominant motif. These lamps are characterised by a wide channel near the top of the nozzle, created by a gradual reduction of decorations on the disc, on which simplified ornaments became increasingly present in time, starting from the 3rd–4th century. In the 5th century, a palmette was often present on this type of lamp, between the nozzle and the disc, which was later replaced by simple channels in variations from the second half of the 6th century (Bjelajac 1990, 186–188). It is believed that these lamps were created as local copies of Corinthian North African lamps, which were also copies, as indicated by the channel between the disc and the nozzle (Curta 2016, 78). Due to multiple stages of copying, the ornaments are often simplified and unclear. Among the late antique pottery lamps made in a mould that belong to local variants, we single out the lamp from the fort of Saldum on the Danube Limes (Jeremić 2009, 138, cat. 403; Ilić, Jeremić 2018, 274–275). The lamp has an oval form with a cross on the disc and geometric motifs on the shoulders. The influence of the late antique tradition is visible on the handle, which is in the form of a stylised palmette (Fig. 5.7). This shape

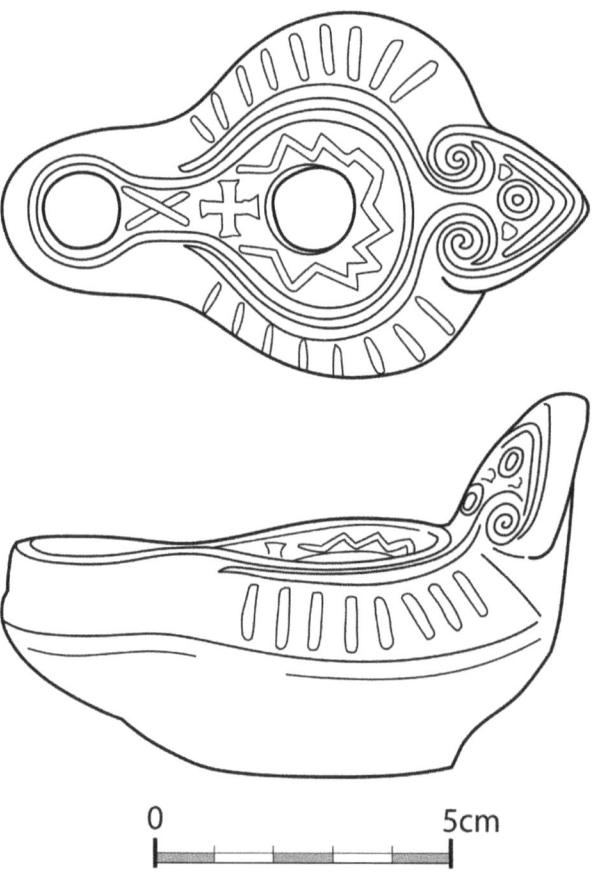

Figure 5.7. Saldum fort. Pottery lamp with a cross and a handle in the form of a palmette. (After: Jeremić 2009, cat. 403).

---

[62] The lamp was found in 1937 in the foundation of the building of the Patriarchate in Belgrade and is housed in the Collection of the Migration Period and the Middle Ages, in the Belgrade City Museum.

Figure 5.8. Prahovo–*Aquae*. Pottery lamp with a cross–shaped handle. (Documentation of the Krajina Museum in Negotin).

of handle is often found in early Byzantine layers, such as a fragmented lamp from Caričin Grad (Bjelajac 1990, 190, pl. XXII/4, XXVI/2) or from Bumbeşti–Jiu, in Romania (Teodor 2001, fig. 6/8).

In the territory of the Danube province of *Dacia Ripensis*, a lamp with a cross-shaped handle was found in *Aquae* – Prahovo. The lamp has an oval form with a cross–shaped handle. The shoulder is decorated with lines, while a stylised star shaped floral ornament is on the disc (Fig. 5.8). It is dated to the 5th century (Janković 1981, 163, T. IX/2). A variant of pottery lamps with a handle in the shape of a cross represents an imitation of popular bronze lamps with a cross-shaped handle (Curta 2016, 86). The main production centres were in the north-eastern part of the Balkans, near the Black Sea (Curta 2016, 87–88). It is possible that the roads through which the Roman army moved from different parts of the Empire represented trade routes at the same time, across which different goods circulated, thus, certain examples of these lamps reached Chersonesus, Near East (Lebanon) or North Africa (Hippo) (Curta 2016, 88–90). The movements of troops from the Balkans may also explain the presence of lamp with cross-shaped handles on the Iron Gate Limes i.e. the city of *Aquae*.

6

Objects of Profane Character with Christian Symbols

6.1. Artistic objects

Statuette of the Good Shepherd

A bronze statuette of the Good Shepherd (*Pastor Bonus*) with a lamb on his shoulders originates from the surroundings of Smederevo (*Vinceia*) (*Konstantin Veliki* 2013, 319, cat. 86; Valtrović 1891b, 109, sl. 1–2). The Shepherd is presented as a young man, with an almost boyish face. His clothing and the fleece of the lamb are crudely represented (Fig. 6.1). This simple and unskilful method of presentation indicates the provincial work of this statuette. The representation of the Good Shepherd is a frequently used motif in Late Antiquity, either as a young man or as an older man with an accentuated beard. Pastoral scenes with philanthropic content were a topic that was often depicted in pagan art. The Old Testament abounds of presentations with the Good Shepherd, for example: David (Psalm 22) and Isaiah (40, 11). In the New Testament, Jesus is a Good Shepherd to believers (John 10, 1–18), with the scene of the return of the lost sheep to its flock (Matthew 18, 12–14; Luke, 15, 4–7). The Good Shepherd represents the relationship between the saviour and those that need to be saved, and this explains his frequent presence in the iconography of Late Antiquity when Christianity became the preeminent and universal world religion (Ilić, Jeremić 2018, 270).

6.2. Jewellery

As an expression of the material and spiritual culture, jewellery has specific traits that vary for members of different ethnic groups. Through jewellery, every individual expresses their need for beauty, and the richness of forms and diversity of decoration techniques bear witness to the general style in the art of a given epoch. Therefore, jewellery that was in use during Late Antiquity can provide precious data on various social processes, typical for this period, as well as the influences of Christianity on the use of decorative motifs.

Necklace

A gold necklace together with a gold ring were found in a grave from the Bela Stena necropolis in the village of Višnjica (*Ad Octavum*), near Belgrade. Two medallions were made in the filigree technique with granulation and a decorative motif in the shape of a palmette. The pendant on the necklace is cross-shaped (Fig. 6.2). Some authors consider that the necklace, in addition to its aesthetic value, also has a deeper symbolic significance (Tatić–Đurić 1964, 193).[63]

According to very close analogies, among which is the finding from Mersin, we can date the necklace to the end of the 5th and the beginning of 6th century (Grabar 1951, 27–49). Some historical circumstances also support this dating. The fortification *Ad Octavum*, one of many that were built or renovated during a period of great building activity, dates to the reign of Justinian I (Barišić 1955a, 67). Most probably, the necropolis next to the fortress, where the necklace was found, also belonged to same period.

Pendants

Pendants in the form of a cross are not common finds from the Danube Limes area during the period of Late Antiquity.

Figure 6.1. Smederevo–*Vinceia*. A statuette of the Good Shepherd. (Documentation of the National Museum of Serbia).

---

[63] For more about this necklace see also: Ilić, Jeremić 2018, 270–272.

Late Antiquity and Early Christianity in the Roman Provinces of Moesia Prima and Dacia Ripensis

Figure 6.2. Višnjica–*Ad Octavum*. Gold necklace with two medallions and a cross. (Documentation of the National Museum of Serbia).

One of such specimen comes from the fort of Ram–*Lederata*. It is decorated with ornaments in the form of concentric circles at the ends of the arms and in the middle of the cross (Vinski 1968, 110–111, T. VII/30). Another cruciform pendant originates from *Viminacium* (Fig. 6.3).[64] It was a part of a necklace with 112 multicoloured beads. The pendat is made of a bronze, and on the front there is a setting, probably for enamel or glass (Ilić, Jeremić 2018, 272). This pendant was found in a child's grave and is dated to the 6th century (Zotović 1994, 66–67).

Three bronze pendants with different forms come from *Romuliana* (Fig. 6.4 a–c). All three of them were discovered in early Byzantine layers, which can be chronologically determined into the 6th century (Janković 1983, 120, kat. 183–185). A bronze cross with a longer vertical arm has a round hole at the top of it, through which it can be attached to a pad. A smaller cross, with approximately equal arms, has a loop at the top of the vertical arm, indicating its function as a pendant. The decoration of this cross consists of a groove, running along the edges of the arms. Another cross-shaped pendant from *Romuliana* contains droplet-shaped extensions at the ends of the arms, characteristic of the 6th century. The decoration was made by casting, and it consists of a series of recesses along the edges of the arms, with triangles and small circles in the middle. The upper arm is missing. All three cross-pendants come from the area of the three-nave basilica, which was dated into the 6th century.

The common feature of all cross-shaped forms of pendants is the fact that they were made of bronze. They are

---

[64] The pendant is a part of the grave inventory (grave no. 134, Više Grobalja site). It makes up a part of the Antiquity collection of the National Museum in Požarevac.

Objects of Profane Character with Christian Symbols

Figure 6.3. Kostolac–*Viminacium*, Više Grobalja site. Pendant in the shape of a cross. (Documentation of the the National Museum in Požarevac).

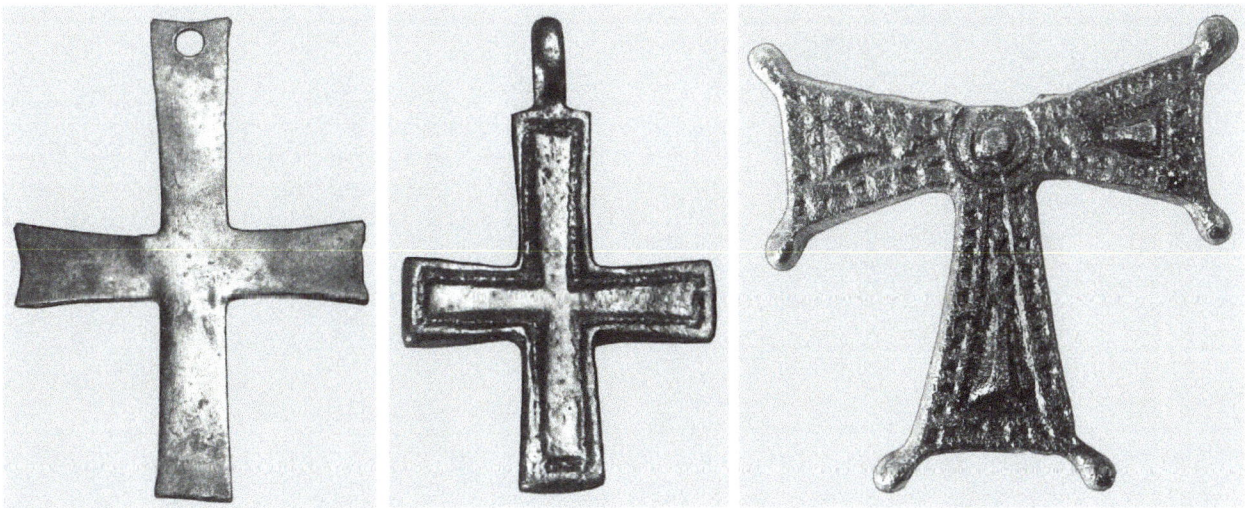

Figure 6.4. a-c Gamzigrad–*Romuliana*. Three cross-shaped pendants. (Documentation of the National Museum in Zaječar).

usually of smaller dimensions, simple and do not display particularly skilful craftsmanship. Decoration most often consists of small concentric circles, which is the ornamental characteristic for Late Antiquity and the early Byzantine period.

Finger Rings

During the Late Antique period, aside from inscriptions with Christian contents, various Christian symbols, first in a hidden manner, and then, from the time of Constantine, openly appeared on rings that were a part of personal jewellery. Thus, the head of a gold finger ring, which is kept at the National Museum in Belgrade, has the inscription IHS, which is an abbreviation for the word "ichthys", the Latin version of the Greek word ιχθύς, meaning "fish" (Popović 2001, kat. 21), (Fig. 6.5). A fish is depicted in a simplified manner, with two curved lines, above the inscription on this ring, while a cross was placed on the lower, inner side of the head of the ring.

53

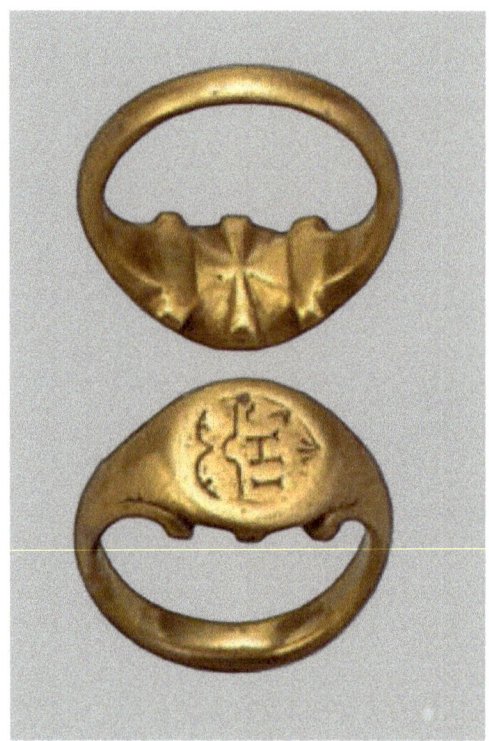

Figure 6.5. Unknown site. Gold finger ring with Christian symbols. (Documentation of the National Museum of Serbia).

Figure 6.6. Kostolac–*Viminacium*, Pećine site. Silver ring with Christogram. (Documentation of the National Museum in Požarevac).

A silver ring from *Viminacium* has a decoration in a form of a Christogram engraved in the head of the ring. The ring is dated to the second half of the 4th century (Fig. 6.6) (Zotović 1994, 65, sl. 5).[65]

In *Viminacium,* in a grave in the necropolis (the site of Pirivoj G/212), among other findings, were found three rings: one with an engraved lion, one with a Christogram, and a third with an unclear image on the head. A bronze coin dated the grave into the middle of the 4th century (Golubović and Korać 2013, 41). Small in number, the Viminacium Christians did not have their own separate necropolis. They buried their dead within Late Roman pagan necropoles. The findings from this grave clearly illustrate the period of religious syncretism that characterized the early period of Christianity.

6.3. Decorative objects of clothing and military equipment

Fibulae

Fibulae can be considered parts of clothing that can have a practical function, but they also reflect the social status of their owner. Such fibulae were a mark of the military or an official honour given by the Emperor on the occasion of state holidays or anniversaries (Petković 2010a, 261). In the territory of the Danube Valley provinces of *Moesia Prima* and *Dacia Ripensis,* no examples of the so-called imperial fibulae have been found – fibulae with inscriptions mentioning certain celebrations. On the other hand, a large number of bronze cruciform fibulae has been discovered, decorated in the niello technique, which sometimes had a Christian mark, with a representation of a Christogram.

The gilded cruciform fibula from Prahovo (*Aquae*) is most probably a part of the grave inventory, together with the previously mentioned gilded glass base made in the *fondi d'oro* technique.[66] The fibula is a well-crafted specimen, with à jour decoration (Fig. 6.7).[67]

This type of fibulae has been found in all parts of the Empire and, judging by the numerous finds, they were well represented along the Danube Limes, particularly in Pannonia.[68] The concentration of such finds along the Danube Limes bears witness to the fact that centres for their productions were also located in this region, and monetary findings that accompanied them indicate that production was at its most intense in the second half of the 4th century (Popović 2009, 103–106).

Applications on Late Antique helmets

The fragments of helmets with Christian symbols shows the level of Christianisation among the Roman troops on the Danube Limes during the period of Late Antiquity (Vujović 2012, 33–38). In *Viminacium*, at the Čair site,

---

[65] Two rings were the grave inventory (child grave no. 213, Pećine site), but today only one is preserved and makes up a part of the Antiquity collection of the National Museum in Požarevac.

[66] The fibula makes up a part of the Late Antiquity collection of the National Museum in Belgrade. In older literature, Dušanovac is stated as the finding place of this fibula, see: Jevremović 1988, 165–169. With a later detailed review of National Museum documentation, it was established that the fibula came into the National Museum in Belgrade through a purchase, together with the previously mentioned gilded glass base (inv. no. 1519/IV).

[67] More about this fibula see: Ilić, Jeremić 2018, 280.

[68] Since the finds are without any clearly defined Christian attribution, we are of the opinion that it is sufficient only to mention some of the sites for a clearer insight into the distribution of these types of fibulae: Ljubljana, Ptuj, Sisak, Osijek, Sremska Mitrovica, Novi Banovci, Dalj, Drnovo.

Figure 6.7. Prahovo–*Aquae*. Bronze cross–shaped fibula with Christogram. (Documentation of the National Museum of Serbia).

in the area of the legionary camp, and from the site of Manastir, a small watchtower in the Iron Gates area on the Danube Limes, parts of decorative applications with a Christogram in relief were found (Fig. 6.8; 6.9).[69]

6.4. Utilitarian objects

Stamps

Since ancient times, bread has had a symbolic meaning and the religious rite of its marking existed before Christianity (Israeli and Merovah eds. 2000, 97). The stamps that were used for marking liturgical bread were usually in the form of a cross. The bronze stamp from *Singidunum* is cross-shaped with an inscription in negative in Greek, Αντονιας καστας, which can be interpreted as "return to Antonius" (Janković 1997, 307, kat. 543; Ilić, Jeremić 2018, 262) (Fig. 6.10).[70]

Weighing equipment

Ancient objects used for measuring, such as weighing equipment like steelyards and counterweights, are relatively rare finds on archaeological sites. A part of a steelyard and a smaller counterweight were found in the area of *Singidunum* (Fig. 6.11a).[71] A counterweight shaped like the bust of a Byzantine empress and a chain system with hooks for hanging loads are also part of this equipment (Fig. 6.11b).[72] Recently, light was shed on the set of circumstances which, more than eighty years ago, led to the separation of the parts of the steelyard (Vujović 2014, 161–183). According to the interpretation of M. Vujović, the steelyard can be aligned with the Constantinople type (Vujović 2014, 169).

On both sides of the beam there is a punched inscription in Greek. The text of both inscriptions begins and ends with a cross:

+ πάπακέσοίκονόμου +

On the other side, there is an inscription, also between two crosses:

+ κύρσφιλ(ικό)ς +

The steelyard from *Romuliana*, province of *Dacia Ripensis*, is similar to the one from Belgrade (Lalović

---

[69] For more detailed description and analysis of these findings see: Ilić, Jeremić 2018, 277–279.
[70] There is no precise data about the finding place of the lamp, except that it was found in the area of Belgrade. It is housed in the Collection of the Migration Period, in the Belgrade City Museum.
[71] The steelyard is a part of the Collection of the Migration Period, in the Belgrade City Museum.
[72] The counterweight shaped like the bust of a Byzantine empress is a part of the Collection of the National Museum of Serbia.

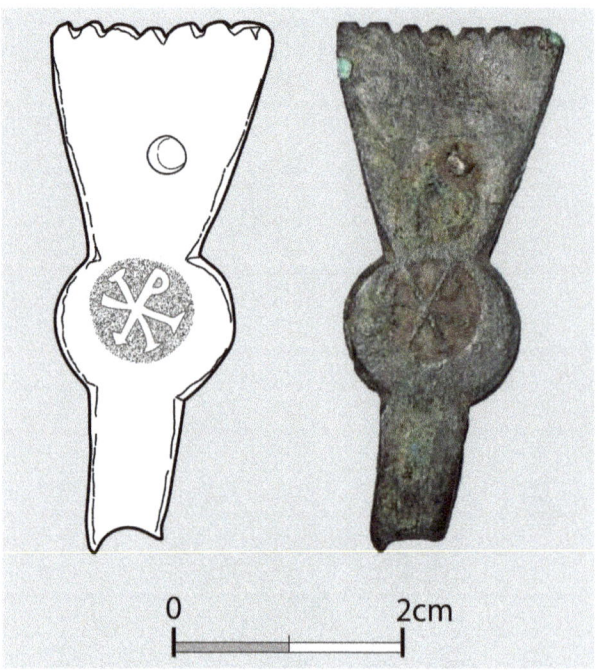

Figure 6.8. Kostolac–*Viminacium*, Čair site. Application of helmet with *Chi-Ro* motif. (After: Vujović 2013, figs. 1/2, 2).

Figure 6.10. Belgrade–*Singidunum*. Bronze stamp in the form of a cross. (Documentation of the Belgrade City Museum).

In the immediate vicinity, steelyards similar to the one from *Singidunum* and *Romuliana* have been found in Caričin Grad (*Iustiniana Prima*) (Bavant *et al.* 1990, 245, Pl. XLIV/299–30), in the early Byzantine fortification in Ras (Popović 1999, 116, sl. 67), and in the fortification in Gradina on Mt Jelica (Milinković 2010, sl. 39–41, T. XIV/5, 60–61). Steelyards of the Constantinople type are generally dated in the period from the 5th to the 7th century. The highest concentration of these finds is in the eastern part of the empire, and inscriptions are mostly in Greek, which indicates that the centre of their production was the Eastern Mediterranean.[73] Parts of a steelyard that was most probably used for the measuring of medicines or precious metals were found in Saldum, a fort on the Danube Limes (Jeremić 2009, 189–190, fig. 89).

The early Christian church in the economic life of the early Byzantine state was important, especially in the hinterlands, away from the main administrative centres and from fiscal control. The steelyard with a counterweight shaped like a Byzantine empress (Ariadne?) from *Singidunum* represents evidence of measures of the Byzantine state, which were undertaken in the context of fiscal organisation and military supply in the hinterlands of the Danube region, from the time of Emperor Anastasius I, and quite certainly during the reign of Justin I and later during the time of Justinian I. Besides the counterweight shaped like the bust of a Byzantine empress, another part of the steelyard from *Singidunum* is a spherical counterweight, which is the weight verified by the exagia kept in the city church (Fig. 11a). Apart from the exagia as the official measure for the weight of gold coins (*exagia solidi*), there were also exagia that were used as a control measure for the weight of the counterweights used in trade (Kostić 1993, 69). They were kept in churches and in that way their accuracy was guaranteed. The steelyard from the early

Figure 6.9. Manastir site, Danube limes. Application of helmet with *Chi-Ro* motif. (After: Vujović 2012, fig. 1/1).

1983, 165, kat. 348). It has a beam with a square cross-section, and measuring units are marked on three sides. Three hooks for different weights were preserved. There are two chains with hooks, on which items would be hung, on the other part of the steelyard. The beam, ending with a biconical button, has a punctuated inscription in Greek with two crosses:

+ Ρουστικίου +

The inscription contains a proper name in the genitive singular case, and it could possibly refer to the person who owned the steelyard. The mobile weight filled with lead and coated with a bronze sheet. The steelyard from *Romuliana* aligned with the Constantinople type.

---

[73] About some more analogies of steelyards of the Constantinople type see: Ilić, Jeremić 2018, 263, 266.

Objects of Profane Character with Christian Symbols

Figure 6.11. a) Belgrade–*Singidunum*. Bronze steelyard and counterweight. (Documentation of the Belgrade City Museum).
b) Belgrade–*Singidunum*. Counterweight shaped like the bust of a Byzantine Empress. (Documentation of the National Museum of Serbia).

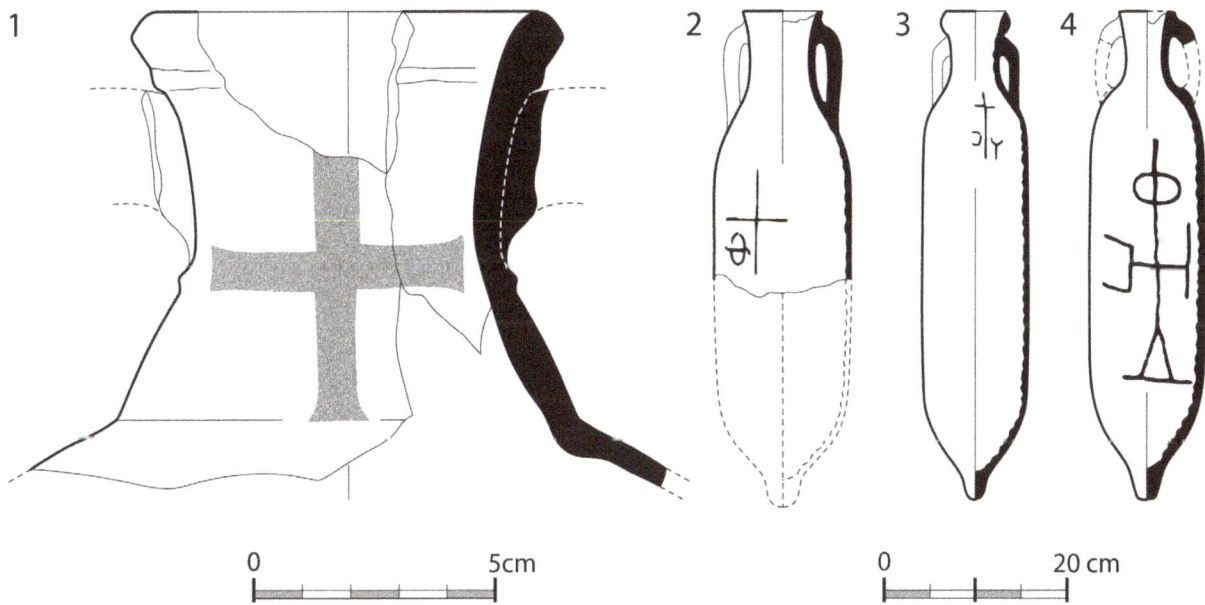

Figure 6.12/1. Saldum fort. Amphora with a cross painted in red. (After: Jeremić 2009, cat. 319). 2, 3. Boljetin–*Smorna*. Amphorae with crosses painted in red. (After: Bjelajac 1996, kat. 167, 168, T. XXXI). 4. Donji Milanovac–*Taliata*. Amphora with cross painted in red. (After: Bjelajac 1996, kat. 174, T. XXXI).

Byzantine fortification of Ras–Podgrađe, which was found on the floor of the 6th century basilica, indicates its purpose (Popović 1999, 116, sl. 67). As previously mentioned, *exagia solidi* were used for the control of weight of gold coins, but they were also used in goldsmithing. Scales and exagia were found in the graves of travelling goldsmiths in Kunszentmárton, Jutas (Hungary) (Kovačević 1977, 167–168, sl. 103, 104). Christian symbols were sometimes represent on the exagia, as was the case with a specimen from Prahovo–*Aquae*, with an acronym, around the cross on the obverse, of *E (clesiae) Mun(di)* (Janković 1981, 166).

Vessels for the storage and transport of food

Amphorae and pithoi are two basic types of vessels that served for the storage and transport of foodstuffs. Sometimes Christian symbols appear on them (Ilić, Jeremić 2018, 275, 277). Amphorae that have a cross painted in red were found in the forts of Saldum (Fig. 6.12/1), Boljetin–*Smorna* (Figs. 6.12/2, 3) and Donji Milanovac–*Taliata* (Fig. 6.12/4). These kinds of objects usually had a long life, so it was common to put marks of ownership on them. In some cases, they were related to the Christian faith of the owner (Bjelajac 1990, 177). The distribution of amphorae directly depended on economic and trade relationships, as well as on the existence of trade routes, more often by sea than by land. In general, they did not belong to local production, but to larger urban structures or trade centres, from where they were distributed as packaging. What is special about these finds is the fact that we cannot put them under any certain chronological criterion, since they were intended for longer use.

7

Funeral Rites

With its dogmatic stances, Christianity brought new elements into the lives of the Romanised population. A belief in the afterlife and the consciousness of the transiency of earthly life in times when people were in so much danger, being attacked and killed, brought courage mixed with religious fanaticism. The worshiping of the dead became even more prominent. The cult of the martyrs sustained and preached the new religion in the first centuries. Martyria were erected, and they would become the gathering places of Christians and focal points from which the new religion would spread. Not only small chapels, but also basilicas were built above the graves of martyrs. These cult places would become centres around which other Christians would be buried as well.

Along with other architectonical activities, urban centres also had to solve the problem of locations for necropoles as well, usually *extra muros*. We encounter almost all types of graves, i.e. funeral architecture, in large Christian necropoles: from built sepulchral chapels of richer believers or those with a higher social rank, built tombs with vaults, built tombs made of bricks or stone, and poor grave pits with wooden caskets. Economic means and social status were also reflected in necropolises. These elements influenced the position and place of burials, since every person of a higher standing would have precedence when it came to being buried within the church or in its immediate vicinity.

Grave monuments also started to be decorated with architectonic ornaments, frescoes that were painted on some tombs walls, relief representations on stone sarcophagi or simple representations of a cross. At first, Christian inscriptions were rather rare, and Christians could be recognised in them through hidden formulas or the added symbol of Christ. Later, when Christianity ceased to be a forbidden religion (*religio illicita*), marking the graves with inscriptions became a frequent occurrence, especially in large necropolises, where a multitude of architectonic monuments and epigraphic inscriptions bear witness to the new religion.[74]

Among the oldest monuments that confirm the presence of Christians in *Singidunum* is a stone sarcophagus with the biblical scene of the Jonah tribulation, the so-called Jonah sarcophagus (Fig. 7.1).[75] There are two scenes on the sarcophagus: on the front side of the Jonah sarcophagus are a representation of the Good Shepherd with a lamb on his shoulders and Biblical scenes from the life of the Old Testament, prophet Jonah. The narration takes place through a series of episodes, with scenes about the suffering and repentance of Jonah. The sarcophagus was decorated with Noric–Pannonian scrolls. The relief is roughly cut and remains only partially finished. It is constructed of limestone and rectangular in shape with a lid in the form of a pitched roof with acroteria at its four corners and one in the middle of the lid's front and back side. The sarcophagus measures 218 x 98 x 74 cm and the lid 229 x 116 x 28 cm.

The first researcher of this sarcophagus Mihajlo Valtrović has correctly suggested that the sarcophagus was probably reused for new burials, most probably in the middle or the second half of the 4th (Valtrović 1891, 142). The scenes of Jonah are among the most commonly reproduced scenes in Late Antique and Early Christian art and appear in reproduced scenes on a variety of objects and settings until the 5th century (Pilipović and Milanović 2016, 222). The sarcophagus from *Singinunum* is a unique example of an early Christian sarcophagus from the area of the Roman Balkan provinces.

The necropolises of Late Antiquity in *Viminacium* developed south from the legionary camp and fortified city.[76] A small number of grave units reliably defined as burials of Christians have been found in *Viminacium*. The burials of rich or respectable Christians are indicated by memorial buildings or fresco-painted tombs. One such painted Christian tomb from the site of Pećine (G/5517) most probably represents a family tomb, with the burials of three men and one woman (Zotović 1994, 64; Korać 1991, 107–122; Korać 2007, 33–68).[77] Symbolic representations with a Christian content were painted on the walls of the tomb. The central motif on the west side is the Christogram in a wreath, made of laurel leaves. To the right and left of the Christogram are the apocalyptical letters α (alpha) and ω (omega) (Fig. 7.2 a-c). The Christogram is a common motif in tomb painting and expresses the hope of eternal life through Christ. In the immediate vicinity, it is found in early Christian tombs in Pécs (*Sopianae*) (Magyar 2009, 107–118) and at the necropolis in Jagodin Mala in Niš (*Naissus*) (Jeremić 2013, 132–133; Rakocija 2009,

---

[74] On this occasion, we will single out several monuments from the 4th century that illustrate, in the best manner possible, the beliefs in the afterlife as preached by the Christian religion.

[75] The sarcophagus was found at the corner of Kapetan Mišina and Jovanova Streets in Belgrade, while digging foundations for a house in 1885. Today it is in the National Museum in Belgrade. About the sarcophagus has been written in numerous articles: Valtrović 1886, 70–71; Valtrović 1891, 130–142, T. 11–12; Petković 1907, 186–219; Pop-Lazić 2002, 21–22, cat. G/116, fig. 9; Pilipović and Milanović 2016, 219–245.

[76] The research of the *Viminacium* necropoles that has taken place since the end of the 19th century and intensively since the 1970s, has yielded data regarding about 13,500 individual or collective burials from the Antiquity and Late Antiquity periods.

[77] The tomb is reconstructed and therefore not in its original location. The presented frescoes are replicas of the originals, which are kept at the National Museum in Požarevac.

Figure 7.1. Belgrade–*Singidunum*. The so-called Jonah sarcophagus. (Documentation of the National Museum of Serbia).

87–105). Besides these two sites, similar decorative settings are found in great numbers in fresco painted tombs, grave panels in the east and west of the Roman Empire (Pillinger 2012, 25–36).

The artist who painted this tomb was obviously well acquainted with Christian dogma, if not a Christian himself, depicting familiar motifs such as the water of life (*aqua vitae*), presented in the form of a kantharos, surrounded with trees of life (*arbor vitae*) and two antithetically positioned peacocks that together symbolise eternal life in paradise (*pax aeterna in paradiso*), but also participation in the Eucharist (Korać 2007, 43–48), (Fig. 7.3). The pictorial symbolism of the tomb indicates the fate of the believer, as an individual, but also the general principles of the new religion. The combination of painted representation and a complex theological message indicates the supreme artistry that presented the Christian dogma in a deeply reflective manner. A coin of Constantine the Great from 307 AD, was found in the grave. Based on the findings and stylist elements of the paintings, the tomb should be dated into the first half of the 4th century.

Members of both the rich and the poor ranks of the urban populations were buried in the pagan necropolis of *Viminacium*. The poor were being buried in simple grave pits or caskets made of already used materials. As grave markings, bricks with inscriptions in Greek or Latin were often used, or only a Christogram (Zotović 1994, 60–67) (Fig. 7.4).

Among the epigraphic monuments we could pay attention are a few tombstones with motives of Christogram or with text displaying Christian character. On one of the of them, funerary inscription engraved on a broken marble slab (36 x 56 x 2 cm). (Fig. 7.5b).[78] The text mentioning certain Marina and her husband Licinius and she is identified in the Christian manner as – *honesta femina*, i.e. honorable woman who respects the Lord. Monument could be classified as early Christian but without closer chronological determination (Mirković 1986, 177, no 217; Gargano 2016, 16). The text goes as follows:

Marina honis / ta femina cultrix / di q(uae)

vixit cum virgi / nio suo an(nis) XXX P. <L>icin (io) 5

Cosanciolo sita es

On one fragmented tegula a significant inscription was found (41 x 55 x 2.5 cm), (Fig. 7.5a). (Mirković 1986, 177, no 216; Gargano 2016, 17). The text is fully preserved goes as follows:

Cristus deus dei / filius custodiat artefices

om / nes qui hoc / [o]pus fecerunt in domino

According to one explanation of that text it is possible that the inscription represents hidden Christian characteristic in some sacred structure, and if that is the case it must has been written before 313 AD (Vulić and fon Premerštajn 1909, 136).

A funerary inscription made of marble found in unknown location has engraved bilingual inscription (40 x 45 x 4 cm)

---

[78] The funerary inscription on marble slab was found in unknown site. It was a part of the Weifert collection in Kostolac, and is currently lost.

Funeral Rites

Figure 7.3. Kostolac–*Viminacium*, the site of Pećine (G/5517). Representation of the Garden of Eden in the painted Christian tomb. (After: Korać 2007, 65).

Figure 7.2. a-c Kostolac–*Viminacium*, the site of Pećine (G/5517). Christogram with the apocalyptical letters α and ω in the painted Christian tomb. (After: Korać 2007, 40).

in Greek and Latin that indicates Christian character by its content (Mirković 1986, 178, no 219; Gargano 2016, 16). In the middle of the tombstone is Christogram separating Greek and Latin text (Fig. 7.5c):

Figure 7.4. Kostolac–*Viminacium*, the site of Pećine. Brick with the engraved Christogram. (After: Spasić-Đurić, 2015, fig. 112).

Figure 7.5. a-d Kostolac–*Viminacium*. Early Christian inscriptions. (After: Mirković 1986, 177, no 216, 217; 178, no 219; 179, no 220).

Οὐαλέριος ἐμῷ Θεοδύ[λῳ. Τόδε μέν μνῆμα

ἐμον●ἥ δέ δόξα σή●μαθ[έτωσαν οὖν παῖδες

τοὺς θρέψαντας φιλ[εῖν●χάριν ἔχω σοι]

καί ζῶν καί ἀναπαυό[μενος διά πα]

5 ντος. Valer(ius) [meo Theodu]

lo. Haec [memoria]

quidem me[a tua autem laus]

Discant igit[ur pueri]

Nutritores a[mare. Gratiam habeo li

10 bi vivus et qu[iescens in perpetuum

A fragment of an inscription found on a limestone slab (36 x 72 x 13 cm) that carries a text in Greek letters introduced by a Christogram inscribed in a circle (Fig. 7.5d), (Mirković 1986, 179, no 220).

XP ΓΡΑ[---]

As we have already pointed out, Christians did not have their separate necropolis in *Viminacium*. They buried their dead within pagan Late Roman necropoles. It is obvious that there was no ban for Christians to be buried among the pagans. Good support of such an assumption is a grave in the necropolis, the site of Pirivoj (G/212). Among other findings, three rings were found: one with an engraved figure of a lion, another with a Christogram, and a third with an unclear image on the head. A bronze coin dated the grave into the middle of the 4th century (Golubović and Korać 2013, 41). There is no doubt that no strict control of regulations had been imposed regarding the burial of Christians in the Danubian provinces of the Roman Empire during the 4th century.

The meeting of paganism and Christianity in *Viminacium*, as a process, began during the 3rd century, under the influence of the newly arrived population from the east, soldiers and merchants who spread new cults (Mithraism or other cults from the sphere of olar theology).[79] After 313 AD, Christians were granted freedom to profess their faith. During the 4th century, Christians continued

---

[79] Zotović Lj. in her monograph discusses the topic of Mithraism, see: Zotović, Lj. *Mitraizam na tlu Jugoslavije*, Beograd 1973.

to bury their dead in the territory of pagan necropolises, often with elements of pagan tradition. This transition from paganism to Christianity probably didn't terminate in 380 AD, when Emperor Theodosius I issued the edict *Cunctos populos*, which proclaimed Christianity to be the main religion in the Roman Empire. This edict didn't mean the end of paganism, which was still practiced and long retained in the conservative strata of the Viminacium population. The evidence for such an assumption is the above-mentioned grave with rings, including one with a Christian symbol.

8

Conclusion

The overview of archaeological monuments from the Danube Valley area, in the Roman provinces of *Moesia Prima* and *Dacia Ripensis*, from the period of the introduction and spread of Christianity, indicates several important points: first, the centres and areas from which Christianity spread, and second, the abundance and character of those monuments that indicate the level of Christianisation, organisation of church domains, influence of liturgical forms on sacral architecture and, finally, the influence this new religion had on the cultural transformation of the Antique world in general. The growing uncertainty, which was primarily the result of frequent barbarian invasions, as well as the conditions caused by the economic crisis that was distressing the empire during the whole of the 3rd century, brought general uncertainty and provided favourable conditions for the spread of messianic ideas among the pagan population, especially those ideas coming from the East.

In the territory of the Balkan Peninsula, Christianity mostly spread from coastal cities of the Adriatic Sea in the west and the Aegean Sea in the east. Thus, in the area of the Roman provinces in the Danube Valley, Christianity mostly spread its influence from Thessaloniki and other Greek cities. The army represented a very important missionary factor, since it arrived from different parts of the Empire, especially the East, and it brought new religious cults to this region, first and foremost Mithraism or other cults from the sphere of solar theology and Christianity. The provenance of these influences left traces on architectonic monuments, decoration and epigraphy. Archaeological remains often speak of the origin of certain influences, with those coming from the East (Syria, Egypt, etc.) especially standing out.

There is not much reliable data on the early spread of Christianity in the area of Northern Illyricum from the period before Diocletian, thus, the existence of Christian communities from this period remains only in the domain of conjecture. As we have already pointed out, the first Christian communities were linked to urban milieux, hence, the existence of cities was, in a way, a precondition for the spread of the new religion. Soldiers from the Roman legions that were arriving from the East, first to the fortifications along the Danube Limes, but also merchants, as an important factor of the economic power of the Empire, were for most part the members of the new religion.

Diocletian's persecutions of the Christians were legitimised with four edicts issued on that occasion, and they had numerous victims in the territory comprehended by the Roman provinces of the Balkan Peninsula. These persecutions indicate the existence of a strong church organisation at the very beginning of the 4th century. Most Christian martyrs registered by the sources or tradition are linked to larger urban centres in the territory of the central Balkans (*Sirmium*, *Singidunum*, *Naissus*, *Remesiana*, *Ulpiana* etc.). A strong church organisation in these urban centres led to the relatively fast spread of Christianity across the territory of Northern Illyricum during the 4th century. Concurrently, this was also a period of harsh Christological discussions and the time of the final formulation of the Christian dogma.

Novelties brought on by the new religion and changes that occurred in the cultural life of the autochthonous Romanised population can best be seen in the architecture and its most common forms. Aside from monumental basilicas, which dominated in every more or less urbanised centre, smaller church edifices were also erected in areas that were more isolated, geographically, from their political and religious centres. According to written sources, episcopacies were formed in the larger cities of the Danube region (*Singidunum*, *Viminacium* and *Aquae*) as early as the 4th century. Unfortunately, the remains of episcopal churches and palaces have not been located to date. Although *Romuliana* did not have the status of a city, basilicas discovered in it so far (two of them had a baptistery), dated into the period from the 5th to the 6th century, indicate the possibility of an episcopal see, according to some authors, however, to date, we have no firm evidence that would support this assumption.

From the times of Justinian I, an obligatory element that appeared in the restored Roman and newly built Byzantine fortifications in the Danube Valley provinces along the Limes – the most fortified border in the area of Northern Illyricum – was a church. The main military centre of the Iron Gates Limes was the fort of *Taliata* – Veliki Gradac, which had a dominant role, in terms of the military, over other fortifications in this part of the Danube Limes. Simultaneously, *Taliata* also became the main church centre in this territory. Within the fortification, a single-nave church was built, with all the elements necessary to perform the rites of the Christian cult, among which was a baptistery with a piscina, with a canopy erected above it. The fortification in Boljetin – *Smorna* also had a single-nave church with a katechoumenon and a baptistery within the naos of the church. In places where building a church within the fortification was not possible due to the configuration of the terrain and narrowed spaces, the needs of soldiers stationed along the Limes were met with a smaller chapel built in one of the towers of the fort, whose shape would be modified and adjusted to the church needs (Saldum, Donje Butorke).

In the larger urban centres, remains of ecclesiastic architecture from the early Christian period are few in numbers. There is no reliable data on early churches from *Singidunum* and *Viminacium*, which is the consequence, on the one hand, of the impossibility to conduct archaeological excavations because of the continuity of habitation all the way up to today (*Singidunum*), but also, on the other hand, of insufficient systematic research activities that would provide more data on this period of development of this two metropoles.

The beginning of the 4th century was the time when Christianity became one of the recognised religions and when Christians acquired the same rights as supporters of other religions in the Roman Empire. Christian symbols are visible on liturgical items, as well as on objects of a profane nature, but we can rarely talk about Christian finds older than the 4th century, if we exclude the bronze lamp from Mezul (*Vinceia*), which is chronologically assigned to the second half of the 3rd century, possibly the beginning of the 4th century. The characteristic of material of the 4th century is the presence of a strong ancient tradition, which is reflected both in the form of the material and in the decorative content. A good example of this is the bronze lamp with the handle in the shape of the head of a griffin from Panjevac near Ćuprija. What defines them as early Christian objects is the individually presented Christian symbols, usually in the form of Christ's monogram (*Chi-Rho*) or the representation of the cross.

The unfavourable political conditions that characterise the 5th century, which are reflected in the incursions of various barbarian tribes into the territory of northern Illyricum, especially the Hun invasion in the middle of the century, are reflected not only in the significantly lower representation of northern Illyricum in ecclesiastical events, but also in the abundance of archaeological material. The consequences of the Hunnic destruction recorded in the sources are also confirmed by the significant reduction or almost complete absence of objects that were used in the Christian cult, and church inventory. The situation is similar with objects of profane purpose, which are significantly less compared to the previous century. The crisis of the Empire was finally overcome at the turn of the 5th to the 6th century. This was followed by a period of restoration both in the material and spiritual spheres, which would reach its peak during the time of Justinian I, the great restorer of the Roman Empire, who made renewed life in the cities once again before the final collapse a few decades later. At the end of the 6th and beginning of the 7th century with the invasion of the barbarian tribes, particularly the Avars and Slavs, the process of the Christianisation of the Romanised indigenous population was interrupted. This discontinuity is evidenced by all the urban structures and fortifications registered thus far, both on the Danube Limes and deeper into the interior of the Balkan Peninsula, all the way to the territory of Greece. In the conquered areas, a new form of life appeared, completely alien to the late antique urban and, already, largely Christianised civilization.

Catalogue

1–5. Chalices (Fig. 3.1)
Silver, casting
H 11.0 cm; dia. of rim 15.5 cm
Kostolac (*Viminacium*)
National Museum of Serbia
5th–6th century

Five identical silver chalices on a high hollow conical foot. The recipients are in the shape of a deep hemispherical bowl. The rims have carved in grooves for lids. Lids of two chalices have been preserved, slightly concave, with fluted edges. There is a cursive inscription engraved into the recess of one of the lids: *matrona*. Another chalice has the same inscription, in cursive, written in the recess of the foot.
Bibliography: Popović 1994, kat. 277–281.

6. Bowl with a Christogram (Fig. 3.2)
Silver, casting, embossing
H 4.6 cm; dia. of rim 13.6 cm
Kostolac (*Viminacium*)
National Museum of Serbia
4th century

A small bowl with a deep, hemispherical recipient, and a wide horizontal rim, decorated with shallow engraved, fluted, parallel lines. The rim is flat, wide, and marked with a string of decorative beads. Christ's monogram (*Chi-Rho*) is engraved in two places, on the lower side of the rim.
Bibliography: Kondić 1994, kat. 276.

7–8. Bowls (Figs. 3.3 a-b)
Silver, casting, stamping
H 5.5 cm; dia. of rim 22.5 cm
H 5.5 cm; dia. of rim 23.7 cm
Kostolac (*Viminacium*)
National Museum of Serbia
5th–6th century

Two almost identical shallow bowls on a foot. There is an embossed circle around the accentuated middle part. On the outer side of the bottom, a rectangular stamp with the motif of the cross was stamped at two opposite ends. The letters *"b"* and "z" are written on both ends of the longer arm of the cross. The letter "z" was interpreted as the beginning of the acclamation *zeses*.
Bibliography: Tatić-Đurić 1967, sl. 1, 2; Kondić 1994, kat. 319–320.

9. Bowl (Fig. 3.4)
Silver, casting, engraving
H 9.5 cm; dia. of rim 20.3 cm
Unknown site
National Museum of Serbia
6th century

A deep bowl, with a thickened rim, and a wide conical foot. There is a monogram on the lower part of the bottom, consisting of Greek letters engraved at the ends of equal-length arms: *z, o, c, a* (*zoca*).
Bibliography: Kondić 1994, kat. 318.

10. Bronze pitcher (Figs. 3.5 a-c)
Bronze; casting, engraving, puncture
H 20.5 cm, dia. of rim 6.5 cm
Kostol (*Pontes*)
National Museum of Serbia
6th–7th century

Pitcher with one handle, with a conical neck, rounded belly and ring-shaped foot. The handle is connected to the brim of the vessel by the wide open jaws of a panther, and to the belly of the vessel by a spear-shaped shield on which there is the head of a ram. On the upper part of the handle a bird is modelled. The surface of the vessel is decorated with incised and punctuated ornaments. On the neck there is an inscription which is a part of the third verse of the 29th Psalm of King David.
Bibliography: Popović 2015, 121–130.

11. Censer (Fig. 3.6 c)
Bronze, casting
H 7.5 cm
Gamzigrad (*Romuliana*)
National Museum, Zaječar
6th century

A hexagonal, bronze censer, with a profiled rim and base. It rests on three feet in the shape of stylised animal paws. There are three eyelets on the rim, with a chain attached at each of them, consisting of figure-of-eight hoops. All three chains are connected with a larger hoop at the top. The sides of the censer are flat, except for one, on which traces of repair can be noted – a rectangular hole, which was closed at a later point.
Bibliography: Janković 1983, kat. 178; Živić 2003, kat. 377.

12. Censer (Figs. 3.7 a-b)
Bronze, casting
H 8.5 cm; dia. of rim 12 cm
Pepeljevac, Kuršumlija
National Museum of Serbia
7th–8th century

A bronze hemispheric censer on a round foot. Chains were attached to the three preserved hoops, which most probably ended under a small circular lid. The censer was decorated in relief representations with Christian motifs. Three ornamental strips can be discerned: an undecorated strip runs along the rim, bordered with decorative ribs

on both sides. There are relief representations of scenes from the life of Christ on the belly of the censer. The third ornamental strip comprehends the part of the foot towards the belly, with a decoration on the rim in the form of a flower with a twenty-petal corolla. The foot is simple and hollow. A seven-petal flower is depicted in the middle of the bottom of the foot.
Bibliography: Ilić 2008, sl. 1; Ljubinković-Ćorović 1950, sl. 2.

13–15. Spoons (Fig. 3.8)
Silver, casting, engraving
L 24.6 cm, 24.3 cm, 24.2 cm
Kostolac (*Viminacium*)
National Museum of Serbia
6th century

Three identical spoons, with an ovoid recipient. There is an engraved monogram – *aenevs* at the spirally profiled transition from the handle to the recipient. The handles of two spoons end with a sharp tip, and the third one has a cone-shaped widening at the end.
Bibliography: Tatić-Đurić 1967, sl. 4; Kondić 1994, kat. 321–322, 324.

16. Spoon
Silver, casting, engraving
L 24.1 cm
Kostolac (*Viminacium*)
National Museum, Požarevac
6th century

The spoon is made in a similar manner to the previous ones, with an ovoid recipient. The handle has a sharp tip at the end.
Bibliography: Tatić-Đurić 1967, sl. 4; Kondić 1994, kat. 323.

17. Spoon
Silver, casting, punching
L 17.0 cm
Gamzigrad (*Romuliana*)
National Museum, Zaječar
5th–6th century

A silver spoon with an ovoid recipient and a spirally profiled transition between the handle and the recipient. The handle narrows towards the end. The inside of the recipient is decorated with a stylised Christogram, made using the punching technique.
Bibliography: Lalović 1983, kat. 346; Kondić 1994, kat. 325.

18. Processional cross (Fig. 3.9)
Bronze, engraving
Dim. 27.0 cm x 21.0 cm
Gamzigrad (*Romuliana*)
National Museum, Zaječar
6th century

A large Latin cross with endings that have circular extensions at the corners of the arms. There is a rich engraved decoration. A band runs along the edges of the arms, with small concentric circles. There are simple rosettes at the ends of the arms and circular extensions, which are alternating, along the centre of the cross, with a stylised floral ornament. A pocket was soldered at the back of the cross, made of thin bronze sheet, used for inserting the handle. The upper arm is missing.
Bibliography: Janković 1983, kat. 182; Živić 2003, kat. 387.

19. Cross – pendant from a processional cross
Lead, casting
Dim. 6.8 cm x 4.4 cm
Kostolac (*Viminacium*)
National Museum of Serbia
6th century

A pendant from a processional cross. The vertical arm has a rounded extension on one side, with a small hole for a hoop.
Bibliography: Marjanović-Vujović 1977, kat. 6.

20. Cross – pendant from a processional cross
Lead, casting
Dim. 7.0 cm x 3.0 cm
Kostolac (*Viminacium*)
National Museum of Serbia
6th century

A part of a processional cross, with extended ends of the arms. There is a semi-circular extension on the upper vertical arm, with a small hole for a hoop. The lower part of the arm is missing.
Bibliography: Marjanović-Vujović 1977, kat. 3.

21. Reliquary (Fig. 4.1)
Silver sheet, embossing, engraving
Dim. 8.8 cm x 5.3 cm x 4.4 cm
Gamzigrad (*Romuliana*)
National Museum, Zaječar
6th century

A reliquary made of rectangular silver sheet. A Latin cross, with arms extended at the ends, was engraved on the front and the back, in a drawn-out rhombus. On the lateral sides, there are fields with incised, slanting, parallel lines. The lid is missing. The reliquary was accidentally discovered outside the northern gate of the fortification.
Bibliography: Živić 2003, kat. 389.

22. Gilded glass base (Fig. 4.2)
Glass with golden foil
Dia. 7.0 cm
Prahovo (*Aquae*)
National Museum, Belgrade
4th century

A base of a vessel, most probably a part of a plate or a shallow bowl with a ring-shaped foot. In a medallion, on a

gold foil, are presented portraits of a man, a woman and a child *en face*. An inscription *vivas in deo* is written above them. The glass is pale green, made in the *fondi d'oro* technique.
Bibliography: Kondić 2005, kat. 109; Ružić 1994, kat. 1194.

23. Polycandelon (Fig. 3.6 a)
Bronze, casting
H 17.9 cm
Gamzigrad (*Romuliana*)
National Museum, Zaječar
6th century

A round polycandelon made of bronze, with four holes for inserting cressets. Four chains were linked at the top with a round plaque. The entire construction was linked, by means of a cross, to a long wire hanging hook.
Bibliography: Janković 1983, kat. 177; Živić 2003, 376.

24. Candelabra (Fig. 3.6 b)
Bronze, casting
H 43.0 cm
Gamzigrad (*Romuliana*)
National Museum, Zaječar
6th century

A candelabra made of bronze, consisting of a stand with three feet, a trunk and a recipient. The stand is in the form of a tripod, with dolphin-shaped ends of the legs, and stylised grapevine leaves in between. The fluted trunk is placed on a profiled base, narrowing towards the top. The recipient is in the shape of a round stylised flower, with a spike for the candle at the centre of it.
Bibliography: Živić 2003, 378; Janković 1983, kat. 179.

25. Mushroom-shaped fittings (Fig. 3.6 d)
Bronze, casting
H 6.2 cm
Gamzigrad (*Romuliana*)
National Museum, Zaječar
6th century

Mushroom-shaped bronze fittings, hollow cast. There is a square recess at the top, with a smaller rectangular hole in the middle, which was the base for an object, most probably a cross. The fittings were located at the top of a stick, belonging to a hoard of church items from the 6th century.
Bibliography: Janković 1983, 135, kat. 180; Živić 2003, 379.

26. Lamp (Fig. 5.2)
Bronze, casting
L 21.0 cm x H 16 cm
Panjevac near Ćuprija
National Museum of Serbia
4th–5th century

A larger bronze lamp with the handle in the shape of the head of a griffin, with a decoratively shaped monogram on it. There is a dove at the top of the monogram. The central part of the wick is decorated on both sides with Christ monograms, with a hole for oil between them. The nozzle of the lamp begins with leaves of acanthus and a decorative ring, and ends in the shape of a stylised nine-petal flower. The foot is small and ring-shaped. There was a hanging hoop on the head of the griffin, and another one at the beginning of the nozzle.
Bibliography: Jeličić 1959, 80–81, T. V/15; Kondić 1993, kat. 145.

27. Lamp (Fig. 5.3)
Bronze, casting
Dim. 14.6 cm x 5.2 cm
Belgrade (*Singidunum*)
Belgrade City Museum
6th century

A bronze lamp with an extended nozzle, and a handle in the shape of a cross. The hole of the oil disc was closed with a shell-shaped lid. The foot has a hole for fastening to a stand, which is missing.
Bibliography: Janković 1997, kat. 578.

28. Lamp (Figs. 5.4, 5.5)
Bronze, casting, engraving
Dim. 41.5 cm x 22.8 cm
Mezul near Smederevo (*Vinceia*)
Museum in Smederevo
3rd–4th century

Lamp in the shape of a boat, with five lateral holes for the flame on each side, in place of the paddles. There is a relief representation of the head of a sea monster at the prow, with a human Fig. shown in its jaws, emerging up to the shoulders, which is interpreted as a representation of Jonah. The sides of the boat are decorated with relief representations of sea fauna (dolphins swallowing smaller fish and octopuses). The prow and the stern of the boat have an engraved votive inscription:

Dei in domu (on the prow)
Tetmogenes votvm fecit (on the stern)

The lid (deck) is missing, as well as the mast and probably a human Fig. at the stern, identical to the one at the prow.
Bibliography: Pavlović 1967, 123–130; Popović 1970, 323–330.

29. Lamp (Fig. 5.6)
Clay, mould
Dim. 12.0 cm x 9.0 cm
Beograd (*Singidunum*)
Belgrade City Museum
5th–6th century

A pottery lamp has an oval shape with an elongated beak. Two figures, male and female, both in the orant position, are presented on the disc. Besides this depiction, crosses

on the disc, beak and a third one on the leg of the lamp indicate the Christian character of the lamp. All three crosses are made of relief dots.
Bibliography: Birtašević 1970, 7–8; Janković 2000, 29-30; Ilić and Jeremić 2018, fig. 20.

30. Lamp (Fig. 5.7)
Clay, mould
Dim. 9.8 cm x 6.0 cm
Saldum fort, Danube Limes
6th century

The lamp has an oval form with an elongated nozzle. The disc has a channel opening towards the nozzle with a representation of a cross, while the wider shoulders are decorated with geometric motifs. The handle is in the form of a stylised palmette.
Bibliography: Jeremić 2009, cat. 403.

31. Lamp (Fig. 5.8)
Clay, mould
Dim. 7.5 cm x 6.9 cm
Prahovo (*Aquae*)
Krajina Museum in Negotin
5th century

The lamp has an oval form with a cross–shaped handle. The shoulder is decorated with lines, while a stylised star shaped floral ornament is on the disc.
Bibliography: Janković 1981, 163, T. IX/2; Ilić and Jeremić 2018, fig. 22.

32. Glass lamp – part of a polycandelon
Glass
H 4.0 cm; dia. 2.7 cm
Gamzigrad (*Romuliana*)
National Museum, Zaječar
4th–5th century

A fragment of the belly and the bottom of a lamp, in a light green colour.
Bibliography: Živić 2003, kat. 108.

33. Glass lamp – part of a polycandelon
Glass
H 7.6 cm; dia. 7.0 cm
Gamzigrad (*Romuliana*)
National Museum, Zaječar
6th century

A glass lamp with a recessed rim and a recessed bottom. There are three cannelures under the rim, and three handles on the belly, used for hanging by means of small hooks. The glass is light green.
Bibliography: Živić 2003, kat. 103.

34. Glass lamp – part of a polycandelon Glass (Fig. 5.1/1)
H 5.2 cm
Gamzigrad (*Romuliana*)
National Museum, Zaječar
6th century

A fragment of the rim and belly of a glass lamp. There is an ornament in the form of slanting parallel cannelures under the rim. The glass is light green.
Unpublished.

35. Glass lamp – part of a polycandelon (Fig. 5.1/2)
Glass
H 1.9 cm
Gamzigrad (*Romuliana*)
National Museum, Zaječar
6th century

A fragment of the bottom of a lamp, with a tubular extension. It was made of light green glass.
Unpublished.

36. Glass lamp – part of a polycandelon (Fig. 5.1/3)
Glass
Dim. 5.0 cm x 4.2 cm
Gamzigrad (*Romuliana*)
National Museum, Zaječar
6th century

A fragment of the rim of a lamp, with an ornament in the form of parallel, horizontal incisions under the rim. The glass is light green.
Unpublished.

37. Glass lamp – part of a polycandelon (Fig. 5.1/4)
Glass
H 2.3 cm
Gamzigrad (*Romuliana*)
National Museum, Zaječar
6th century

A fragment of a glass lamp, with a narrowed bottom.
Unpublished.

38. Glass lamp – part of a polycandelon
Glass
Dim. 2.2 cm x 3.0 cm
Gamzigrad (*Romuliana*)
National Museum, Zaječar
6th century

A fragment of the rim of a lamp, made of light green glass.
Unpublished.

39. Statuette (Fig. 6.1)
Bronze, casting
H 7.2 cm
Vicinity of Smederevo
National Museum of Serbia
4th century

A statuette of the Good Shepherd with a lamb on his shoulders. The details of the face and the clothes are given

only in a simplified manner. The lower parts of the legs of the Shepherd are missing.
Bibliography: Valtrović 1891, 109, sl. 1–2; Kepeski 1969, kat. 300.

40. Necklace (Fig. 6.2)
Gold, casting, perforation, filigree, granulation
L of the chain 34.0 cm; dia. of the large medallion 2.38 cm;
Dia. of the small medallion 1.18 cm
Višnjica (*Ad Octavum*)
National Museum of Serbia
5th–6th century

A gold necklace with a cross and two medallions. The chain is made of large, alternately linked hoops. The gold cross is at the free end of the chain, hanging on a small hook used for fastening. The double medallions, intended to be the front decoration, were made using the filigree and granulation technique. The edge of the medallion is adorned with granules. The small medallion, which is fastened to the larger one, is identical in its decorative details to the central part of the larger medallion. There are four reduced palmettes on it, made using the filigree technique.
Bibliography: Tatić-Đurić 1964, T. I/1; Popović 2001, 92, sl. 27.

41. Pendant (Fig. 6.3)
Bronze, casting
Dim. 2.6 cm x 1.4 cm
Kostolac (*Viminacium*)
The site of Više Grobalja G/134
National Museum, Požarevac
6th century

A pendant in the shape of a cross, made of thick bronze sheet. There is a base on the front, most probably for a piece of enamel that fell off. The cross was a part of a necklace consisting of 112 colourful beads.
Bibliography: Zotović 1994, 66, sl. 6.

42. Pendant
Bronze, casting
Dim. 4.5 cm x 2.8 cm
Ram (*Lederata*)
National Museum, Belgrade
6th century

A pendant in the shape of a cross, decorated with an ornament in the shape of concentric circles, at the end of the arms and in the middle of the cross.
Bibliography: Vinski 1968, 110-111, T. VII/30.

43. Pendant (Fig. 6.4 a)
Bronze, casting
Dim. 6.0 cm x 4.0 cm
Gamzigrad (*Romuliana*)
National Museum, Zaječar
6th century

A bronze cross with a long vertical arm. There is a round hole at the end of the vertical arm, used for fastening to a base.
Bibliography: Janković 1983, kat. 183.

44. Pendant (Fig. 6.4 b)
Bronze, casting
Dim. 4.3 cm x 2.9 cm
Gamzigrad (*Romuliana*)
National Museum, Zaječar
6th century

A small cross, with arms of approximately equal length, and a loop near the end of the vertical arm. Its decoration consists of a groove running along the edge of the arms.
Bibliography: Janković 1983, kat. 184.

45. Pendant (Fig. 6.4 c)
Bronze, casting
Dim. 3.1 cm x 1.9 cm
Gamzigrad (*Romuliana*)
National Museum, Zaječar
6th century

A bronze cross with drop-shaped extensions at the end of the arms. The decoration is made in the casting technique, and consists of a series of recesses along the edge of the arms, with triangles and circles in the middle. The upper arm is missing.
Bibliography: Janković 1983, kat. 185.

46. Finger ring (Fig. 6.5)
Gold, casting, engraving
Dia. 2.2 cm
Unknown site
National Museum of Serbia
4th century

Elegant gold finger ring of a simple shape with Christian symbols engraved on the flat, circular head, decorated with two curved lines (fish) above the inscription IHS (ichthys – fish) on top side of the head and an engraved cross in relief on the underside of the ring head.
Bibliography: Popović 2013, kat. 125.

47. Finger ring (Fig. 6.6)
Silver, casting, engraving
Dia. 1.9 cm
Kostolac (*Viminacium*)
The site of Pećine G/213
National Museum, Požarevac
4th century

Silver ring with rectangular decorative head. *Chi-Ro* motif is engraved on it.
Bibliography: Zotović 1994, 65, sl. 5.

48. Finger ring
Bronze, casting, engraving
Dia. 2.2 cm

Kostolac (*Viminacium*),
The site of Pirivoj G/212
Documentation Centre, Viminacium
4th century

A bronze finger ring with a Christogram engraved on a flat head.
Bibliography: Golubović and Korać 2013, 41, fig. 5.

49. Fibula (Fig. 6.7)
Bronze, gold plate, casting, engraving, niello.
Dim. 8.7 cm x 4.7 cm
Prahovo (*Aquae*)
National Museum of Serbia
4th century

A large cross-shaped fibula with gilding, and highly profiled, large bulbs. It has a richly decorated wide bow and foot with engraved ornaments, filled with niello. The central part of the foot is decorated with a fishbone motif, made using the engraving and niello technique. There is an ornament along the edge of the foot in the form of a half-rotated Latin letter "C". There is an identical ornament on the highly placed bow. Christ's monogram *Chi-Rho* is carved into the end of the rectangular foot. The transversal arm has large bulbs at the ends. The pin is missing.
Bibliography: Jevremović 1988, 165-169, sl. 1, 2; Popović 2001, cat. 89.

50. Application with *Chi-Ro* motive (Fig. 6.8)
Bronze, casting
L 4.7 cm
Legionary camp (*Viminacium*)
Documentation Centre, Viminacium
4th century

A part of a decorative application of Late Late Antique helmet with a *Chi-Ro* motif.
Bibliography: Vujović 2012, 33 figs. 1/2, 2.

51. Application with *Chi-Ro* motive (Fig. 6.9)
Copper, gold plate
l 2.3 cm
The site of Manastir, Danube Limes
4th century

A decorative application with gilded surface and *Chi-Ro* motif on the front side of the halmet.
Bibliography: Vujović 2012, 33 fig. 1/1.

52. Stamp (Fig. 6.10)
Bronze, casting
Dim. 10.7 cm x 10.2 cm
Belgrade (*Singidunum*)
Unknown site
Belgrade City Museum
4th century

A cross-shaped bronze stamp for marking liturgical bread. The cross, with arms of almost equal length, has a Greek inscription on it, cast in negative, $ANT\Omega NIA\Sigma\ KA\Sigma TA\Sigma$. The remains of the original handle are on the back.
Bibliography: Janković 1997, 325, kat. 543.

53. Steelyard with two counterweights (Figs. 6.11 a-b)
Bronze, casting, engraving, punching
L 61.2 cm
Spherical counterweight 120.15 g
Counterweight shaped like the bust of a Byzantine Empress
H 13.4 cm, 1551 g
Belgrade (*Singidunum*)
Unknown site (Dubrovačka Street ?) Belgrade
Belgrade City Museum, National Museum of Serbia
6th century

Weighing equipment: a part of a steelyard, a beam with a measuring scale with a punched inscription, counterweight shaped like the bust of a Byzantine Empress and a smaller counterweight, found in Belgrade (*Singidunum*). On both sides of the shorter part of the beam of the steelyard there is a punched inscription in Greek. The text of both inscriptions begins and ends with a cross:

$+ πάπακέσοίκονόμου +$

On the other side, part of the text, also between two crosses, may be read as:

$+ κύρσφιλ(ικό)ς +$

Besides the counterweight shaped like the bust of a Byzantine Empress, which was made using the hollow casting technique, with its cavity partly filled with lead, another part of the steelyard from Belgrade is a fully cast spherical counterweight.
Bibliography: Janković 1997, 333, kat. 577; Vujović 2014, 166–167, sl. 4–7.

54. Steelyard with counterweight
Bronze, casting, engraving, embossing
L 35 cm
Gamzigrad (*Romuliana*)
National Museum, Zaječar
6th century

A part of a steelyard, a beam with a measuring scale with an embossed inscription, and mobile weight filled with lead and covered with a bronze sheet found in *Romuliana*. Three hooks for different weights have been preserved. The beam, which ends with a biconical knob, has an embossed inscription in Greek:

$+ Ρουστικίου +$

Another part of the steelyard is a fully cast spherical counterweight.
Bibliography: Lalović 1983, 165, kat. 348.

55. Weight
Bronze

Weight 4.56 g (preserved only as a drawing)
Prahovo (*Aquae*)
6th century

A bronze weight with an abbreviation on the front side:

E (clesiae) Mun(di) +

There is a cross with a monogram on the reverse, containing the letters *a, n i, v* and *s*, which can be either interpreted as *Annius* or *Asinius*.
Bibliography: Janković 1981, 166.

56. Amphora (Fig. 6.12/1)
Baked clay
Dia. of rim 9.0 cm
Saldum fort, Danube Limes
6th century

Fragmented neck and shoulder of an amphora, made of reddish baked clay. On the neck is a red-brown painted cross.
Bibliography: Jeremić 2009, 113, cat. 319.

57. Amphora (Fig. 6.12/2)
Baked clay
H 35.0 cm
Boljetin fort (*Smorna*), Danube Limes
6th century

A fragment of the neck, belly and handle. There is a motif of a cross, in red, on the upper part of the belly. The Greek letter θ can be noted in the lower right corner, enclosed by the arms of the cross.
Bibliography: Bjelajac 1996, 89, kat. 168.

58. Amphora (Fig. 6.12/3)
Baked clay
H 51.0 cm
Boljetin fort (*Smorna*), Danube Limes
6th century

An amphora, preserved whole, made of well refined clay, of light red colour. There is a motif with the representation of a cross, in red, on the shoulder.
Bibliography: Bjelajac 1996, 89, kat. 167.

59. Amphora (Fig. 6.12/4)
Baked clay
H 51.0 cm
Veliki Gradac fort (*Taliata*), Danube Limes
6th century

A fragment of an amphora. The rim, a part of the neck and a part of the handle are missing. There are Greek letters, in red, on the belly.
Bibliography: Bjelajac 1996, 89, kat. 174.

60. Amphora
Baked clay
H 43.5 cm
Ravna fort (*Campsa*), Danube Limes
6th century

An amphora with a profiled rim and thin fluted handles. The letter "m", with a cross on the ligature, is on the belly, written in red.
Bibliography: Zotović and Kondić 1978, 219, kat. 218.

61. Amphora
Baked clay
The site of Mokranjske Stene, near Negotin
Museum of Krajina, Negotin
6th century

A fragment of an amphora with horizontal ribs. An inscription in Greek, with Christian content, was preserved:

Α + Ω Χ(ριστον) Μ(αρία) γ(εννα) [.....].

Bibliography: Janković 1981, 154, sl. 65/b.

62. Amphora
Baked clay
Dim. 11.2 cm x 11.7 cm
Gamzigrad (*Romuliana*)
National Museum, Zaječar
6th century

A fragment of a small spindle-shaped amphora with an inscription with Christian content, written in Greek:

Φ + Σ – [Ι(ησονς) Χ(ριστός)] /Φ(ώς) Σ(ωτήρ).

The amphora is of light colour, while the inscription is in dark red.
Bibliography: Lalović 1983, 165, kat. 349.

63. Amphora
Baked clay
Dim. 9.0 cm x 5.5 cm
Gamzigrad (*Romuliana*)
National Museum, Zaječar
6th century

A fragment of an amphora with accentuated rib-shaped shoulders, in pink. There is an inscription, in red-brown:

+ ΧΜG/Ω +Χ(ρστον) Μ(αρία) Γ(εννά) / [Α] Ω.

As with the previous case, this text reveals the Christian character of the vessel.
Bibliography: Lalović 1983, 165, kat. 350.

64. Pithos
Baked clay
L 4.5 cm
Gamzigrad (*Romuliana*)
National Museum, Zaječar
6th century

A fragment of the rim of a pithos, in a red hue, with a recessed and flattened rim. There is an equal-armed cross carved on it.
Bibliography: Janković 1983, 132, kat. 160.

65. Pithos
Baked clay
L 13.2
Gamzigrad (*Romuliana*)
National Museum, Zaječar
6th century

A fragment of the rim of a pithos, with a stamp, in the form of a circle with a cross in the middle. It was made of well refined earth, in dark grey.
Unpublished.

66. Pithos
Baked clay
L 8.5 cm
Gamzigrad (*Romuliana*)
National Museum, Zaječar
6th century

A fragment of the rim of a pithos, with an engraved ornament in the shape of a cross. The pithos is grey, made of well refined earth.
Unpublished.

67. Pot
Baked clay
L 13.3 cm
Gamzigrad (*Romuliana*)
National Museum, Zaječar
6th century

A fragment of the rim of a pot, with an engraved motif in the shape of an equal-armed cross.
Bibliography: Živić 2003, kat. 71.

68. Bowl
Baked clay
H 8.0 cm
Gamzigrad (*Romuliana*)
National Museum, Zaječar
5th–6th century

A fragment of the rim and the belly of a large, deep bowl. There is a decoration on the rim, in the form of four circular stamps with a cross. There are two unskilfully engraved crosses in-between the stamps. The bowl is of a brown-grey colour.
Bibliography: Janković 1983, sl. 107 kat. 162.

69. Base of jug
Baked clay
Dia. of base 12.0 cm
Saldum fort, Danube Limes
6th century

The base of jug made of red-brown baked clay. A Christogram was symmetrically engraved on the base before baking.
Bibliography: Jeremić 2009, fig. 59, cat. 337.

70. Jug
Baked clay
L 6.0 cm
Gamzigrad (*Romuliana*)
National Museum, Zaječar
6th century

A fragment of the handle of a jug, in the form of a strip. A cross was applied at the junction point with the belly of the vessel. The vessel was made of baked clay, in grey-yellow colour.
Unpublished.

71. Plating
Bone
Dim. 5.7 cm x 2.3 cm
Karataš fort (*Diana*), Danube Limes
4th century

A rectangular item – panel decorated on both ends with the motif of a net, and a cross in the middle.
Bibliography: Petković 1995, kat. 690, T. XLI/7.

72. Plating
Bone
Dim. 4.5 x 2.0 cm
Gamzigrad (*Romuliana*)
National Museum, Zaječar
6th century

A bone plaque, partially damaged, which was a segment of bone plating. It is decorated along the edges with parallel lines and rhombi, and there is an ornament in the shape of a cross in the middle, which has circles, with a dot in the middle, at the end of the arms.
Unpublished.

73. Sarcophagus (Fig. 7.1)
Limestone, carving
Dim. 2.18 x 0.98 x 0.74 m
Belgrade (*Sinigidunum*)
National Museum of Belgrade
4th century

The sarcophagus is constructed of limestone, rectangular in shape with a lid in the form of a pitched roof with acroteria. On the front of the sarcophagus is a rectangular field, with lateral edges decorated with Noric-Pannonian volutes. The sarcophagus depicts scenes from the life of Jonah, the Old Testament prophet: there are two figures rowing and one tossing Jonah overboard into the jaws of a sea monster; in the middle are depicted a tree, sea monster throwing out Jonah onto the dry land and a Fig. of a dolphin; the left field has a dominant standing Fig. of the Good Shepherd, with a lamb around his neck.

Bibliography: Valtrović 1886, 70–71; Valtrović 1891, 130–142, T. XI–XII; Pop-Lazić 2002, 21–22, G–116, fig. 9; Pilipović and Milanović 2016, 219–233, fig. 1–2.

74. Christ monogram (Figs. 7.2 a-c)
Fresco–painted Christian tomb
Dim. 1.65 and 0.63 x 1.54 m
Kostolac (*Viminacium*)
The site of Pećine (G/5517)
Museum in the site of Viminacium
4th century

Early Christian painted tomb. The central motif on the west side is the Christogram in a wreath made of laurel leaves. To the right and left of the Christogram are the apocalyptical letters α (alpha) and ω (omega).
Bibliography: Korać 2007, 33–42.

75. The Garden of Eden (Fig. 7.3)
Fresco–painted Christian tomb
Dim. 1.67 x 0.73 and 1.52 m
Kostolac (*Viminacium*)
The site of Pećine (G/5517)
Museum in the site of Viminacium
4th century

Early Christian painted tomb. The representation of the Garden of Eden with peacocks and a Kantharos between, surrounded with trees of life (*arbor vitae*).
Bibliography: Korać 2007, 43–48.

76. Roman brick (Fig. 7.4)
Baked clay
Kostolac (*Viminacium*)
National museum, Požarevac
4th century

A rectangular brick with the engraved Christogram, as a grave marking.
Bibliography: Zotović 1994, 61; Spasić-Đurić, 2015, fig. 112.

77. Christian inscriptions (Fig. 7.5 a-d)
Kostolac (*Viminacium*)
4th century

Early Christian inscriptions from *Vimincium*.
Bibliography: Mirković 1986, 177, no 216, 217; 178, no 218, 219.

Ancient Sources

Aug. *Genesi.* – Augustini, *De Genesi ad litteram,* in: *Corpus Scriptorum Ecclesiasticorum Latinorum* Vol. 28, part 1, (ed.) J. Zycha, Wien 1894.

Clem. *Paedag.* – Clementis Alexandrini, *Paedagogus*, in: *ANF, Vol. 2*, (transl.) W. Wilson, (eds.) A. Roberts, J. Donaldson, A. Cleveland, Buffalo 1885.

Lact. *Mort. Pers.* – Lactantius, *De mortibus persecutorum*, ed. and transl. by J. L. Creed, Oxford 1984.

Lib. Pont. – Liber Pontificalis in: *The Book of Pontiffs (Liber Pontificalis): The Ancient Biographies of the First Ninety Roman Bishops to AD 715*, (transl.) R. Davis, Liverpool 2000.

Migne, *PL* – J. P. Migne, *Patrologiae cursus completus.* Series Latina, Paris 1844–1864.

Not. dign. – *Notitia dignitatum: pars Occidentis; pars Orientis; accedunt Notitia urbis Constantinopolitanae et Laterculi provinciarum,* (ed.) Otto Seeck, Berlin 1876 (rp. Frankfurt am Main), 1962.

Nov. XI – Iustinianus, *Nov. XI*, transl. by F. H. Blume, http://www.uwyo.edu/lawlib/blume-justinian/ajc-edition-2/novels/index.html.

Paulini, *Poem X* – Paulini, *Poemata X Ausonio Paulinus* in: *The Poems of St. Paulinus of Nola, Ancient Christian Writers,* vol. 40, (transl.) P. G. Walsh, New York- Paramus 1975.

Procop. *De Aedif.* – Procopius *De Aedificis,* in: *Buildings* (transl.) H. B. Dewing, London 1940.

Bibliography

Badawy, A. 1978. *The Art of the Christian Egyptians from the Late Antique to the Middle Ages*. Cambridge, Mass. and London: MIT Press.

Barišić, F. 1955a. *Vizantijski izvori za istoriju naroda Jugoslavije* I. Beograd: Filozofski fakultet.

Barišić, F. 1955b. "Vizantijski Singidunum". *ZRVI* 3: 1–14.

Baumstark, von R., ed. 1998. *Rom und Byzanz. Schatzkammerstücke aus bayerischen Sammlungen*, Katalog zur Ausstellung des Bayerischen Nationalmuseums. München: Bayerisches Nationalmuseum.

Bavant, B. 1990. "Les petits objects". In *Caričin Grad II: Le Quartier Sud-est de la Ville Haute*, edited by B. Bavant, V. Kondić, J. M. Spieser, 191–257. Belgrade and Rome: L'école française de Rome and Institut Archéologique.

Bénazeth, D. 1992. *L'art du métal au début de l'ère chrétienne*, Catalogue du département des antiquities égyptiennes. Paris: Musée du Louvre.

Bierbrauer, V. 1975. *Die ostgotischen Grab-und Schatzfunde in Italien*. Spoleto: Centro italiano di studi sull'alto Medioevo.

Birtašević, M. 1955. "Jedan vizantijski žižak iz arheološke zbirke Muzeja grada Beograda". *Godišnjak GB* 2: 43–46.

Birtašević, M. 1970. *Srednjovekovna keramika*, Beograd.

Bjelajac, Lj. 1990. "La céramique et les lampes". In *Caričin Grad II: Le Quartier Sud–est de la Ville Haute*, edited by B. Bavant, V. Kondić, J. M. Spieser, 161–190. Belgrade and Rome: L'école française de Rome and Institue of Archaelogy.

Bjelajac, Lj. 1996. *Amfore gornjomezijskog Podunavlja*. Beograd: Arheološki institut.

Bouras, L. and Parani, M. 2009. *Lighting in Early Byzantium*. Washington: Dumbarton Oaks Research Library & Collection.

Bratož, R. 2003. "Dioklecijanovo preganjanje kristijanov v provincah srednjega Podunavja in zahodnega Balkana". In *Mednarodni znanstveni simpozij ob 1700-letnici smrti Viktora Ptujskega*, edited by S. Kranjc, 29–98. Ptuj: Minoritski samostan Sv. Viktorina.

Brenk, B. 2003. *Die Christianisierung der spätrömischen Welt*. Wiesbaden: Reichert.

Bugarski, I. and Ivanišević, V. 2013. "Ranosrednjovekovna ostava gvozdenih predmeta iz Rujkovca i slučajni nalazi sa područja centralnog Balkana". *Starinar* 63: 131–152.

Buschhausen, H. 1971. *Die spätrömischen Metallscrinia und frühchristichen Reliquiare*. Wien.

Cabrol F. and Leclercq, H. 1907–1953. *Dictionnaire d'archéologie chrétienne et de liturgie*. Paris.

Cambi, N. 1976. "Neki kasnoantički predmeti od stakla s figuralnim prikazima u Arheološkom muzeju u Splitu". *AV* 25: 139–157.

Cermanović-Kuzmanović, A. 1976. "Pregled i razvitak rimskog stakla u Crnoj Gori". *AV* 25: 175–190.

Cermanović–Kuzmanović, A. 1979. "Rimsko utvrđenje kod Kladova". *Starinar* 28–29: 127–134.

Cruiskshank Dodd, E. 1961. *Byzantine Silver Stamps*. Washington: Dumbarton Oaks Research Library & Collection.

Curta, F. 2016. "Shedding Light on a Murky Matter: Remarks on 6th to Early 7th Century Clay Lamps in the Balkans". *Археология българика* 3: 51–116.

Čanak-Medić, M. 1978. *Gamzigrad kasnoantička palata*, Beograd: Republički zavod za zaštitu spomenika kulture.

Dalton, O. M. 1901. *Catalogue of Early Christian antiquities and objects form the Christian East*. London.

Diehl, E. 1961. *Inscriptiones latinae christianae veteres*, vol. II, Berolini.

Guyon, J. and Heijmans, M. eds. 2001. *D'un monde à l'autre. Naissance d'une Chrétienté en Prvence IVe –VIe siècle*. Catalogue de l'exposition. Arles: Musée de l'Arles.

Du Bourget, P. 1970. *Umetnost Kopta*: Novi Sad: Bratstvo jedinstvo.

Evans, A. 1883. *Antiquariens Researches in Illyricum* IV, Westminster.

Faccani, G. 2012. "Die Anfänge des Christentums auf dem Gebiet der heutigen Schweiz bis ins 4. Jahrhundert". In *Christianisierung Europas. Entstehung, Entwicklung und Konsolidierung im archäologischen Befund. Internationale Tagung im Dezember 2010 in Bergisch–Gladbach*, edited by O. Heinrich–Tamáska, N. Krohn, S. Ristow, 97–120. Regensburg: Schnell & Steiner.

Ferjančić, S. 1997. "The Prefecture of Illyricum in the 4th Century". *Mélanges d'histoire et d'épigraphie*, (offerts à Fanoula Papazoglou): 231–239.

Ferjančić, S. 2013. "Istorija rimskih provincija na tlu Srbije u doba Principata". In *Konstantin Veliki i Milanski edikt 313*, edited by I. Popović and B. Borić-Brešković, 26–35. Beograd: Narodni muzej.

Foltiny, S. 1974. "Spätrömische und wölkerwanderungszeitliche Slilberlöffel aus der alten

Welt im Metropolitan Museum of Art in NY". *Situla* 14/15: 263–268.

Fülep, F. 1984. *Sopianae. The History of Pécs during the Roman Era, and the Problem of the Continuity of the Late Roman Population*. Budapest: Akadémia Kiadó.

Gabra, G. 1996. *Kairo: Das Koptische Museum und die frühen Kirchen*. Kairo. Egyptian Internat. Publ. Company–Longman.

Gargano, I. 2016. Evidence of Christianity in Viminacium: a study on historical sources, epigraphy, and funerary art". *Studia Academica Šumensia* 3: 11–29.

Gerke, F. 1973. *Kasna antika i rano hrišćanstvo*. Novi Sad: Bratstvo jedinstvo.

Golubović, S. and Korać, M. 2013. "Grave Inventory – a Reflection of the Belief of Deceased". *Tibiscvm, s.n. Arheologie* 3: 37–43.

Gonosová, A. and Kondoleon, Ch. 1994. *Art of Late Rome and Byzantium*. Richmond: Virginia Museum of Fine Arts.

Grabar, A. 1951. "Un médaillon en or provenant de Mersine en Cilicie". *Dumbarton Oaks Papers* 6: 27–49.

Grünbart, M. 2006. "Byzantine Metal Stamps in a North American Private Collection". *Dumbarton Oaks Papers* 60: 13–24.

Grupa autora. 1980. *Od arheološkoto bogatstvo na SR Makedonija*, katalog izložbe, Skopje.

Hartley, E., Hawkes, J., Hening, M. and Mee, F. eds. 2006. *Constantine the Great, York's Roman Emperor*, York: York Museums and Gallery Trust.

Ilić, O. 2008. "Early Christian Baptistries in Northern Illyricum". *Starinar* 56: 223–244.

Ilić, O. 2011. "Early Christian Imports and Local Imitations of Imported Goods in the Territory of the Central Balkans". In *The Roman Empire and Beyond: Archaeological and Historical Research on the Romans and Native Cultures in Central Europe*, edited by E. C. De Sena and H. Dobrzanska, 35–50. Oxford: BAR International Series 2236.

Ilić, O. and Jeremić, G. 2018. "Early Christian Finds on the Middle Danube Limes". In: *Vivere militare est. From Populus to Emperors – Living on the Frontier*, Volume I, edited by S. Golubović and N. Mrđić, 247–290, Belgrade: Institute of Archaeology.

Israeli, Y. and Mevorah, D. eds. 2000. *Cradle of Christianity*. Catalogue of the Exhibition. Jerusalem: The Israel Museum.

Janković, Đ. 1981. *Podunavski deo oblasti Akvisa*, Beograd: Arheološki institut.

Janković, Đ. 1983. "Ranovizantijski Garmzigrad". In *Gamzigrad kasnoantički carski dvorac*, edited by S. Ćelić, 120–142. Beograd: Galerija SANU.

Janković, M. 1997. "Seoba naroda". In *Antička bronza Singidunuma*, edited by S. Krunić, 305–340. Beograd: Muzej grada Beograda.

Jeličić, B. 1959. "Bronzani žišci u Narodnom muzeju". *Zbornik radova NM* 2: 73–82.

Jeličić, B. 1964. "Bronzani kandelabr u Narodnom muzeju u Beogradu". *Zbornik NM* 4: 151–155.

Jeremić G. 2009. *Saldum. Roman and Early Byzantine Fortification*. Belgrade: Institute of Archaeology.

Jeremić, G. 2013. "The late antique necropolis in Jagodin Mala, Niš (Naissus), Serbia – eight years of research". In *Strategie e Program mazione della Conservazione e Trasmissibilità del Patrimonio Culturale*, edited by A. Filipović and W. Troiano, 272–281. Roma: Edizioni Scientifiche Fidei Signa.

Jeremić, G. 2013. "Sahranjivanje u kasnoj antici u Naisu – primer nekropole u Jagodin Mali". In *Konstantin Veliki i Milanski edikt 313*, edited by I. Popović and B. Borić-Brešković, 126–135. Beograd: Narodni muzej.

Jeremić, G. and Ilić O. 2018. "Evidence of Early Christianity on the Danube Limes, from Singidunum to Aquae". In: *Vivere militare est. From Populus to Emperors – Living on the Frontier*, Volume I, edited by S. Golubović and N. Mrđić, 197–246, Belgrade: Institute of Archaeology.

Jeremić, M. 1995. "Balajnac, agglomération protobyzantine fortifiée". *Antiquité tardive* 3: 193–207.

Jevremović, N. 1988. "Krstasta fibula sa Hristovim monogramom iz Narodnog muzeja u Beogradu". *Zbornik NM* 13–1: 165–169.

Jovanović, A. 1975. "Krstoobrazne fibule iz antičke zbirke Narodnog muzeja u Nišu". *Zbornik NM* 8: 235–245.

Jovanović, A. 1978. *Nakit u rimskoj Dardaniji*. Beograd: Savez arheoloških društava Jugoslavije.

Jovanović, A. 1984. "Hajdučka Vodenica, kasnoantičko i ranovizantijsko utvrđenje". *Starinar* 33–34: 319–331.

Kanitz, F. 1892. *Römische Studien in Serbien. Der Donau-Grenzwall, das Strassennetz, die Städte, Castelle, Denkmale, Thermen und Bergwerke zur Römerzeit im Königreiche Serbien,* Wien: Tempsky.

Kartašov, A. V. 1995. *Vaseljenski sabori* I. Beograd: Srpska književna zadruga.

Kaufman, C. M. 1913. *Handbuch der christlichen Archäologie*. Paderborn: Schöningh.

Khatchatrian, A. 1962. *Les baptistères paléochrétiens*. Paris: École Pratique des Hautes Études.

Kent, J. P. C. 1961. "The Comes Sacrarum Largitionum, (Ex.)". In *Byzantine Silver Stamps*, edited by E. C. Dodd, 35–45. Washington: Dumbarton Oaks Research Library and Collection.

Kondić, J. 1994. "Ranovizantijsko srebro". In *Antičko srebro u Srbiji*, edited by I. Popović, 65–67. Beograd: Narodni muzej.

Korać, M. 1995. "Srebrna kašika iz kasnoantičkog utvrđenja kod Ljubičevca". In *Radionice i kovnice srebra*", edited by I. Popović, T. Cvjetićanin, B. Borić–Brešković, 189–196. Beograd: Narodni muzej.

Korać, M. 1991. "Late Roman Tomb with Frescoes from Viminacium". *Starinar* 42: 107–122.

Korać, M. 2007. *Slikarstvo Viminacijuma*. Beograd: Centar za nove tehnologije Viminacium.

Kostić, Z. 1993. "Prilozi uz ranovizantijsku metrologiju". *Glasnik SAD* 9: 67–77.

Kovačević, J. 1977. *Avarski kaganat*. Beograd: Srpska književna zadruga.

Khroushkova, L. 1981. "Les baptistères paléochrétiens du littoral oriental de la Mer Noir". *ZRVI* 20: 15–24.

Lebreton, J. et Zeiller, J. 1946. *L'Eglise primitive* I. Paris: Bloud & Gay.

Lalović, A. 1983. "Epigrafski spomenici". In *Gamzigrad, kasnoantički carski dvorac*, edited by S. Ćelić, 163–170. Beograd: Galerija SANU.

Ljubinković-Ćorović, M. 1950. "Stara kadionica iz okoline Kuršumlije". Muzeji 5: 70-86.

Lybenova, V. 1981. "Selišteto ot rimskata i rannovizatijska epoha". *Pernik* 1: 107–203.

Mano-Zisi, Đ. 1962. "Stukatura u Stobima" *Zbornik radova NM* 3: 101–107.

Marjanović–Vujović, G. 1973. "Dva rana hrišćanska polijeleja Narodnog muzeja". *Zbornik NM* 7: 13–23.

Marjanović-Vujović, G. 1977. *Krstovi od VI do XII veka iz zbirke Narodnog muzeja*. Beograd: Narodni muzej.

Marjanović-Vujović, G. 1983. "Bokal sa grčkim natpisom". In *Arheološko blago Srbije – iz muzejskih zbirki*, edited by D. Krstić, M. Veličković, G. Marjanović-Vujović, 117, kat. 98. Beograd: Narodni muzej.

Marjanović-Vujović, G. 1987. "Pontes – Trajanov most, Srednjovekovna ostava V". *Đrdapske sveske / Cahiers des Portes de Fer* 4: 135–142.

Marsigli, L. F. 1726. *Danubius pannonico-mysicus observationibus geographicis, astronomicis, hidrographicis, historicis, phisicis perlusreatus*. Hague–Amsterdam: Cmitum, apud P. Grosse, R.C. Alberts, P. de Hondt – Uytwerf & Changuion.

Magyar, Z. 2009. "The world of late antique Sopianae: artistic connections and scholarly problems". In *Niš and Byzantium* 7, edited by M. Rakocija, 107–118. Niš: Univerzitet u Nišu.

Migotti, M. 2003. *Pozlaćena stakla sa Štrbinaca kod Đakova*. Đakovo: Muzej Đakovštine.

Milinković, M. 1986. "*Ranovizantijska utvrđenja u unutrašnjosti Srbije*". master's thesis, Univerzitet u Beogradu.

Milinković, M. 2010. *Gradina na Jelici*. Čačak: Narodni muzej.

Milojčić, V. 1970. "Zu den spätkaiserzeitlichen und merowingischen Silberlöffeln". *Bericht der RGK* 49: 111–133.

Milošević, G. 2017. "Porodični mauzolej u selu Brestovik kod Beograda". *Saopštenja* XLIX: 7–23.

Minchev, A. 2003. *Early Christian reliquaries from Bulgaria (4th–6th century AD)*. Varna: Varna Regional Museum of History.

Minić, D. 1984. "Manastir, praistorijsko, antičko i srednjovekovno nalazište". *Starinar* 33–34: 153–157.

Mirković, L. 1965. *Pravloslavana liturgika ili nauka o bogosluženju pravoslavne istočne crkve*. Beograd: Sv. Arhij.

Mirković, M. 1976. *Inscriptions de la Mésie Supérieure* I,.Singidunum et son territoire". In *Inscriptions de la Mésie Supérieure* I, edited by F. Papazoglou, 21–92. Beograd: Centre d'etides épigraphiques et numismatiques.

Mirković, M. 1979. "Licinije i progoni hrišćana u Singidunumu". *Zbornik FF* 14-1: 21-27.

Mirković, 1981. "Balkanske oblasti u doba poznog carstva". In *Istorija srpskog naroda*, knj. 1, edited by S. Ćirković, 89–104. Beograd: Srpska književna zadruga.

Mirković, M. 1986. *Inscriptions de la Mésie Supérieure II: Viminacium et Margum*. Beograd: Centre d'etides épigraphiques et numismatiques.

Mirković, M. 1995. "Episcopus Aquensis and Bonosiacorum scelus". In. *The Age of Tetrarchs*, edited by D. Srejović, 205–216. Belgrade: Galerija SANU.

Mirković, M. 2006. *Sirmium, istorija rimskog grada od I do kraja VI veka*. Sremska Mitrovica: Blago Sirmijuma.

Mottier, I. and Bosson, N. 1989. *Les Kellia: Ermitage coptes en Basse-Egypte*, exhibition catalogue: Genève: Musée d'art et d'histoire.

Mundell Mango, M. 1986. *Silver from Early Byzantium: the Kaper Koraon and Related Treasures*. Baltimore: Walters Art Gallery.

Mundell Mango, M. 1998. "The Archaeological Context of Finds of Silver in and beyond the Eastern Empire". In *Acta XIII Congressus Internationalis Archaeologiae Christianae,* Pars II, 207–252. Città del Vaticano – Split.

Nesbitt, J. W. 1988. *Byzantium: The Light in the Age of Darkness*. New York.

Ostrogorski, G. 1959. *Istorija Vizantije*. Beograd: Prosveta.

Papazoglu, F. 1957. *Makedonski gradovi u rimsko doba*. Skopje: Živa Antika.

Pavlović, L. 1967. "Rimska bronzana lucerna oblika ratnog broad". *Starinar* 17: 123–130.

Petković, S. 2010a. *Rimske fibule u Srbiji od I do V veka*. Beograd: Arheološki institut.

Petković, S. 2010b. "Romulijana u vreme posle carske palate". In *Felix Romulina – Gamzigrad*, edited by I. Popović, 167–199. Beograd: Arheološki institut.

Petković, V. 1907. "Jedan rani hrišćanski sarkofag iz Beograda". *Glas SKA* 72: 186–219.

Petrović, P. 1976. *Niš u antičko doba*. Niš: Gradina.

Petrović, P. 1984. "Saldum, rimsko i ranovizantijsko utvrđenje na ušću potoka Kožica". *Starinar* 33–34: 128–134.

Pillinger, R. 2012. "Early Christian Grave Paintings in Niš between East and West". In: *Niš and Byzantium* 10, edited by M. Rakocija, 25–36. Niš: Univerzitet u Nišu.

Pilipović, S. and Milanović, Lj. 2016. "The Jonah Sarcophagus from Singidunum: A Contribution to the Study of Early Christian Art in the Balkans". *Classica et Christiana* 11: 219–245.

Popović, I. 1994. "Produkcija srebra u periodu ranog carstva: lokalni proizvodi i import". In *Antičko srebro u Srbiji*, edited by I. Popović, 45–54. Beograd: Narodni muzej.

Popović, I. 2001. *Kasnoantički i ranovizantijski nakit od zlata u Narodnom muzeju u Beogradu*. Beograd: Narodni muzej.

Popović I. 2009. "Gilt Fibula with Christogram from Imperial Palace in Sirmium". *Starinar* 57: 101–112.

Popović, I. 2013. "Nakit kao insignija vlasti, carska donacija i privatni ukras". In *Konstantin Veliki i Milanski edikt 313*, edited by I. Popović and B. Borić-Brešković, 188-195. Beograd: Narodni muzej.

Popović, I. 2015. "Bronze flagon from Pontes with an inscription form the 29th Psalm of David". *Starinar* 65: 121–130.

Popović, I. and Popović, A. 2003. "Greek inscription on golden Finger ring from National Museum in Belgrade". *Starinar* 52: 157–161.

Popović, J. 1912 (rp. 1995). *Opšta crkvena istorija* I, Novi Sad: Romanov.

Mano Zisi, Dj., Veličković, M., Jeličić B. 1969. *Antička bronza u Jugoslaviji*. Beograd: Narodni muzej.

Popović, M. 1999. *Tvrđava Ras*, Beograd: Arheološki institut.

Popović, R. 1991. "Beogradski mučenici Ermil i Stratonik". *Bogoslovlje* 1–2: 73–80.

Popović, R. 1995. *Rano hrišćanstvo na Balkanu pre doseljenja Slovena*, Beograd: Teološki fakultet.

Popović, V. 1967. "Uvod u topografiju Viminacijuma". *Starinar* 18: 29–53.

Popović, V. 1970. "Ranohrišćanska bronzana lampa iz okoline Smedereva". *Starinar* 20: 323–330.

Popović, V. 1984. "Donji Milanovac – Veliki Gradac (Taliata), rimsko i ranovizantijsko utvrđenje". *Starinar* 33–34: 265–282.

Popović, V. "Grčki natpis iz Caričinog Grada i pitanje ubikacije Prve Justinijane". *Glas SANU* CCCLX, knj. 7: 53–108.

Rădulescu, A. and Lungu, V. 1989. "Le christianisme an Scythie Mineure à la lumière des dernière découvertes archéologiques". *Actes du XIe Congrès International d'Archéologie Chrétienne,* vol. III, Città del Vaticano: École française de Rome: 2561–2615.

Rakocija, M. 2009. "Painting in the crypt with an anchor". In *Niš and Byzantium* 7, edited by M. Rakocija, 87–105. Niš: Univerzitet u Nišu.

Rankov, J. 1983. "Kasnoantičko stakleno dno ređeno u tehnici fondi d'oro". *Zbornik NM* 11–1: 85–89.

Rizos, E. 2015. "Martyrs from the north-western Balkans in the Byzantine ecclesiastical tradition: patterns and mechanisms of cult transfer". In *Forschungen zu Spätantike und Mittelalter*, edited by O. Heinrich-Tamaska, N. Krohn and S. Ristow, Band 4, 195–213. Remshalden: Bernhard Albert Greiner.

Ross, M. 1960. "Byzantine Bronze Peacock Lamps". *Archaeology Summer* vol. 13, no 2: 134–136.

Ross, M. 1962. *Catalogue of the Byzantine and Early Mediaeval Antiquities in the Dumbarton Oaks Collection*, vol. I, Washington: Dumbarton Oaks Research Library and Collection.

Ružić, M. 1994. *Rimsko staklo u Srbiji*. Beograd: Univerzitet u *Beogradu*, Filozofski Fakultet.

Shukriu, E. 1989. "Fortifikata Hisar ne Kasterc të Suharekës". *Iliria* 19–1: 77–85.

Simoni, K. 1988. "Srebrna žlica iz Siska". *VAMZ* 21: 79–86.

Spätantike und frühbyzantinische Silbergefässe aus der Staatlichen Ermitage Leningrad. Ausstellung der Staatlichen Ermitage Leningrad in der Frühchristlich-byzantinischen Sammlung der Staatlichen Museen zu Berlin. Berlin: Staatlichen Museen.

Spasić-Đurić, D. 2015. *Grad Viminacijum*. Požarevac: Narodni muzej Požarevac.

Srejović D. and Cermanović-Kuzmanović, A. 1992. *Rečnik grčke i rimske mitologije*, Beograd: Srpska književna zadruga.

Stiegemann Ch., ed. 2001. *Byzanz das Licht aus dem Osten. Katalog der Ausstellung.* Paderborn: Erzbischöflichen Diözesanmuseum.

Stryzgowski, J. 1904. *Koptische Kunst.* Catalogue du Musée du Caire. Vienne: Imprimerie Adolf Holzhausen.

Šukunda, M. 2017. "*Verska politika Rimskog carstva od 311–380. godine*". PhD diss., University of Belgrade.

Tatić-Đurić, M. 1960. "Jedna kasnoantička lampa iz zbirke Narodnog muzeja u Beogradu". *ŽA* 10: 237–248.

Tatić-Đurić, M. 1962. "Bronzani teg sa likom vizantijske carice". *Zbornik NM* 3: 115–126.

Tatić-Đurić, M. 1964. "Zlatni nalaz iz Višnjice". *Zbornik NM* 4: 185–192.

Tatić-Đurić, M. 1967. "Srebrno posuđe iz Kostolca". *Zbornik NM* 5: 237–246.

Teodor, D. Gh. 2001. "Christian Roman Byzantine Imports North of the Lower Danube". *Interacademica* 2–3: 118–130.

Tešić-Radovanović, D. 2018. "*Predstavljanje svetlosti. Simbolika ukrasa ranohrišćanskih svetiljki sa prostora centralnog Balkana (IV-VII vek)*". PhD diss., University of Belgrade.

Tošić G. and Rašković, D. 2009. "Hrišćanski motivi na arheološkom materijalu iz okoline Kruševca i Aleksinca". In *Niš i Vizantija* 7, edited by M. Rakocija, 179–195. Niš: Univerzitet u Nišu.

Truhelka, Ć. 1931. *Starohrišćanska arheologija.* Zagreb: Hrvatsko književno društvo sv. Jeronima.

Valtrović, M. 1886. "Starohrišćanski sarkofag nađen u Beogradu". *Starinar* 3: 70–71.

Valtrović, M. 1891a. "Starohrišćanski mrtvački kovčeg nađen u Beogradu". *Starinar* 8: 130–142.

Valtrović, M. 1891b. "Dobri pastir". *Starinar* 8: 109–130.

Vasić, M. 1907. "Nekolike grobne konstrukcije iz Viminacijuma". *Starinar* n.r. 2: 66–98.

Vasić, M. 1984. "Čezava – Castrum Novae". *Starinar* 33–34: 91–122.

Vasić, M. 1995. "Le limes protobyzantin dans la province de Mésie Première". *Starinar* 45–46: 41–53.

Vinski, Z. 1968. "Krstoliki nakit epohe seobe naroda u Jugoslaviji". *VAMZ* 3: 103–168.

Vujović, M. 2012. "Few contributions on the Late Roman helmets from Iron Gate". *Vesnik VM* 39: 29–43.

Vujović, M. 2014. "Ranovizantijski kantar iz Beograda". *Starinar* 64: 161–183.

Vulić, N. and fon Premerštajn, A. 1909. "Antički spomenici u Srbiji". *Spomenik SANU* 47: 109–191.

Zečević, E. 2013. "Srbija i Vizantija: Glas Gospodnji nad vodama vaskrsnuća". In *Narodni muzej: Zlatni presek*, edited by A. Starović, B. Borić-Brešković, T. Cvjetićanin, E. Zečević, 232–233: Beograd: Narodni muzej.

Zeiller, J. 1918, (rp. Roma 1967). *Les origines chrétiennes dans les provinces danubiennes de l'Empire romain*, Roma: L'Erma di Bretschneider.

Zotović, Lj. 1973. *Mitraizam na tlu Jugoslavije*, Beograd: Arheološki institut.

Zotović, Lj. 1984. "Boljetin (Smorna), rimski i ranovizantijski logor". *Starinar* 33–34: 211–225.

Zotović, Lj. 1986. "Južne nekropole Viminacija i pogrebni obredi". *Viminacivm* 1: 41–60.

Zotović, Lj. 1994. "Die Gepidische Nekrople bei Viminacium". *Starinar* 43–44: 183–190.

Zotović, Lj. 1994a. "Rano hrišćanstvo u Viminacijumu kroz izvore i arheološke spomenike". *Viminacium* 8–9: 59–72.

Živić, M. 2003. *Felix Romuliana: 50 godina odgonetanja.* Zaječar: Narodni muzej u Zaječaru.